What We Choose To Build

Who Holds Power, Who Bears Risk, and How Real Estate Decisions Shape Society

SUHAIL Y TAYEB

Printed in the United States of America

A NOTE TO THE READER

This book is designed to be used, not just read.

The frameworks, systems, and case logic presented here are meant to support real decisions about land, power, policy, and the long-term impacts of real estate development. It is a guide for anyone seeking to understand how decisions are made in real estate and how those decisions shape cities, communities, and opportunities.

For readers who want a deeper, guided exploration of how these ideas are applied in practice, a companion video series is available separately. These sessions expand on the material in the book and focus on how real estate professionals, investors, and policymakers navigate the tradeoffs, power dynamics, and governance challenges that determine what gets built, where, and for whom. Full transcripts are provided with the video series so that the material can be reviewed, searched, and revisited over time.

Additional information about the companion materials is available at www.SuhailYTayeb.com

For readers facing complex real estate, social, or governance decisions, seeking independent strategic guidance, further resources, and contact information are also available there.

DEDICATION

For those who make decisions that shape lives.

And for my brother Sameer,
who stepped in when decisions mattered most,
asked the hard questions that expose risk and accountability,
and made sure the system held when others couldn't.

TABLE OF CONTENTS

PREFACE

This book starts with a simple observation that too often gets ignored.

Most of the forces shaping our cities, our buildings, and our lives are not abstract. They are the product of decisions. Decisions about land. Decisions about capital. Decisions about who gets protected, who gets displaced, and who gets heard.

For years, sustainability in real estate has been reduced to checklists. Energy use. Carbon intensity. Certifications. These matter. But they are not the whole story. They never were.

What gets built, where it gets built, and for whom it gets built is ultimately a question of power. Power exercised through zoning codes and financing terms. Through governance structures, regulatory choices, and institutional rules that quietly determine what counts as risk and what counts as value.

Too many conversations about sustainability stop short of that reality. They remain comfortable. They stay technical when the outcomes are deeply human. They stay neutral when the consequences are anything but. This book was written to push past that avoidance.

I wrote this for students, professionals, investors, policymakers, and anyone trying to make sense of why well-intentioned projects so often fall short, and why others quietly succeed. It is not a manifesto. It is a framework. A way of seeing how history, policy, finance, governance, and design interact as one system.

You will not find easy answers here. Cities do not offer them. What they offer instead are patterns, tradeoffs, warnings, and openings. Learning to read those signals is the difference between reacting to change and shaping it. If you are looking for certainty, this is not that book. If you are looking for clarity, it is.

Suhail Y Tayeb

SECTION 1: THE FOUNDATION

HEADS UP AND STRIVE: FRAMEWORKS FOR PEOPLE & POWER

When sustainability is discussed in real estate, the conversation often moves quickly to technical measures. Energy use. Carbon emissions. Certifications. These matter, but they leave out two forces that ultimately determine outcomes. The people affected by real estate decisions and the systems that decide how those decisions get made.

Real estate development operates inside a web of competing interests. Developers, policymakers, investors, architects, and communities rarely share the same incentives. Rules collide. Certifications do not always align with zoning codes or financing terms. Community needs often sit uncomfortably alongside return targets.

In this environment, good intentions are not enough. What is missing is structure. Frameworks help impose discipline on complexity without pretending it can be eliminated. They help surface tradeoffs, expose blind spots, and connect outcomes to decision-making.

This chapter introduces two frameworks I developed for that purpose. HEADS UP and STRIVE.

HEADS UP: Social Impact
HEADS UP is a way to organize how people fit into sustainability decisions. It stands for Housing Affordability, Economic Access, Access to Health, Data Security, Skills and Human Capital, Urban Equity, and Public Infrastructure.

H: Housing Affordability asks whether people can live securely in the places where they work and contribute. It is not only about rent levels or mortgage costs, but about long-term stability and displacement risk.

E: Economic Access looks at who can participate in sustainable development. Financing tools such as PACE, green bonds, or tax credits shape access in ways that are often invisible but decisive.

A: Access to Health includes both healthcare infrastructure and building-level conditions such as air quality, daylight, thermal comfort, and noise. These factors shape daily life far more than most performance reports acknowledge.

D: Data Security has become unavoidable as buildings grow smarter. Sensors, access systems, and digital platforms generate personal data. Who owns it, who protects it, and how it is used are now social questions, not just technical ones.

S: Skills and Human Capital ask whether projects create pathways for workers. Training, safety, and long-term career development determine whether sustainability produces opportunity or simply shifts risk.

U: Urban Equity focuses on distribution. It asks whether projects reduce or reinforce existing inequalities tied to race, income, and geography.

P: Public Infrastructure reminds us that no building functions alone. Water, power, transportation, broadband, and emergency services are shared systems. Resilience depends on their strength and governance.

HEADS UP reframes sustainability as human well-being, not just efficiency.

STRIVE: Governance and Accountability
STRIVE focuses on how decisions are made. It examines whether sustainability commitments are embedded in governance or confined to messaging.

STRIVE stands for Strategy, Transparency, Resilience, Innovation, Values, and Ethics.

S: Strategy asks whether sustainability is integrated into long-term objectives or treated as a side initiative.

T: Transparency examines what is disclosed, how it is measured, and whether stakeholders can meaningfully evaluate performance. This is where greenwashing often hides.

R: Resilience looks at preparedness. It asks how organizations plan for shocks such as market volatility, regulatory shifts, climate risk, or reputational damage.

I: Innovation considers whether organizations adapt. This includes technology, partnerships, financing structures, and governance reforms.

V: Values ask who ultimately benefits. They test whether decisions create durable, shared value or prioritize short-term gains.

E: Ethics examine how decisions are justified. Fairness, integrity, and responsibility are not abstract ideals. They shape trust and long-term viability.

STRIVE provides a lens to evaluate whether governance supports sustainability or undermines it.

Putting HEADS UP and STRIVE Together

HEADS UP and STRIVE work best together. HEADS UP focuses on outcomes for people and communities. STRIVE focuses on the structures and incentives that produce those outcomes.

A project can perform well technically and still fail HEADS UP if it displaces residents or ignores health. An organization can publish ambitious goals and still fail STRIVE if accountability is weak or incentives are misaligned.

Used together, these frameworks separate surface-level sustainability from durable impact.

Why This Matters

Clients, regulators, and investors increasingly demand more than emissions data. They want evidence of fairness, resilience, and accountability.

HEADS UP and STRIVE provide a common language to evaluate decisions, challenge assumptions, and explain tradeoffs. They connect people, power, and performance.

Most importantly, they help answer the question that matters most in real estate. Not just what is being built, but who it serves, who decides, and who bears the consequences.

WHY GOOD INTENTIONS FAIL WITHOUT ACCOUNTABILITY

History is full of warnings that were visible long before they became crises.

In the 1930s, farmers plowed up vast stretches of the Great Plains. Native grasses that held fragile soil in place were replaced with crops on land that received less than ten inches of rain a year. When drought arrived, there was nothing left to anchor the ground. Winds lifted the soil into the air and carried it across states. The Dust Bowl was not a surprise. It was a slow failure of judgment that unfolded in plain sight.

The energy crises of the 1970s followed a similar pattern. So did Cape Town's water crisis in 2018. In each case, risks were known, data existed, and warnings were available. What failed was not information. What failed was accountability.

That pattern matters for real estate.

What ESG Is and What It Is Not

ESG stands for Environmental, Social, and Governance. It is often misunderstood, politicized, or overstated. At its core, ESG is a reporting framework. It does not tell anyone what to do. It does not embed judgment. It does not make decisions.

ESG functions like a medical report. It measures conditions. It reports indicators. It presents risk factors. What happens next depends entirely on the patient, or in this case, the organization, the investor, or the regulator. A medical report does not force you to exercise more or eat fewer donuts. It simply reports the consequences of your choices.

ESG works the same way. It reports exposure, performance, and risk.

ESG in Real Estate

In real estate, ESG reporting describes how assets are developed, operated, and governed. It covers environmental exposure such as energy use, water risk, and materials. It reports social conditions such as housing affordability, workforce practices, and data security. It documents governance structures such as board oversight, transparency, and ethical controls.

What ESG does not do is resolve tradeoffs. It does not decide whether a project should move forward. It does not weigh profit against displacement or efficiency against equity. That work belongs to people and institutions.

Confusing ESG with a decision framework leads to frustration and false expectations. ESG reveals conditions. Accountability determines outcomes.

When Accountability Fails

The costs of ignoring reported risks are well documented.

Volkswagen installed software to cheat emissions tests. The data existed. Governance failed. In real estate, the Chinese drywall scandal exposed homes to sulfur gases that corroded wiring and harmed residents. Materials were specified. Oversight failed.

These were not failures of measurement. They were failures of decision-making.

Social Reporting and Real Outcomes

The same logic applies to social outcomes.

In 1967, more than 1,800 low-income families were displaced from Manhattan's Lower East Side with promises of new housing that never arrived. ESG-style reporting would have captured displacement risk. What failed was governance. Decades later, Essex Crossing emerged only after accountability was forced back into the process.

The High Line tells a different story. Reporting helped reveal value creation, but governance decisions determined who benefited and who was priced out. ESG did not choose the outcome. People did.

Reporting surfaces impact. Governance determines response.

Governance Is the Deciding Factor

Enron collapsed not because the numbers were unavailable, but because leadership hid them. Kobe Steel falsified materials data for years. Contracts existed. Oversight failed. Governance failures convert known risks into real harm.

This is why governance sits at the center of ESG reporting. Without accountability, transparency becomes decoration.

ESG Beyond the Myths

ESG is often dismissed as virtue signaling or praised as a cure-all. Both views miss the point. ESG is about visibility. It makes risks legible. It does not neutralize them.

Organizations that treat ESG as a substitute for judgment tend to perform poorly. Organizations that use ESG to inform difficult decisions tend to endure.

Efficiency, safety, fairness, and resilience are not political positions. They are operational realities.

ESG and Sustainable Development

Sustainable development is a normative goal. It asks what kind of future we want. ESG is a reporting mechanism. It asks what conditions exist today.

Confusing the two leads to category errors. ESG does not deliver sustainability. It reports alignment or misalignment with stated goals.

Materiality analysis helps prioritize what gets reported. It does not absolve decision makers of responsibility for what they choose to ignore.

What ESG Actually Enables

When used properly, ESG gives investors, regulators, and operators a shared language to assess risk and performance. It allows comparison. It enables scrutiny. It supports accountability.

It does not replace leadership.

The leaders who succeed are rarely ideological. They are attentive. They read the data. They recognize vulnerabilities. They understand that reporting only matters if someone is willing to act on what it reveals.

Good intentions fail when accountability is absent. ESG does not fix that problem. It makes it visible.

SECTION 2: MEASURING IMPACT

GLOBAL GOALS AND LOCAL TRADEOFFS

At the turn of the millennium, leaders from 189 countries agreed on an ambitious premise. Extreme poverty was not inevitable. In 2000, that belief became the Millennium Development Goals, a set of eight targets aimed at improving living standards within fifteen years.

The results were real. Extreme poverty was cut in half. Child mortality declined sharply. Access to education and basic healthcare expanded. More than a billion people were lifted out of the most severe forms of deprivation.

But the limits were just as clear. Inequality persisted. Environmental degradation accelerated. Gender disparities remained entrenched. Hundreds of millions of people still lived without reliable access to food, water, or opportunity.

The lesson was not failure. It was scope.

From MDGs to SDGs

In 2012, the UN Conference on Sustainable Development in Rio recognized that poverty, inequality, environmental stress, and institutional weakness could not be treated as separate problems. That recognition led to the Sustainable Development Goals, adopted in 2015 and implemented in 2016.

The SDGs expanded the frame. Seventeen goals. One hundred sixty nine targets. A universal agenda that applied to all countries, not just developing ones. Governments, businesses, and cities were all explicitly included.

The SDGs do not prescribe solutions. They define conditions that must be addressed if development is to be durable.

The SDGs embody the UNs' vision of sustainability: "meeting the needs of the present without compromising the ability of future generations to meet their own needs."

The Sustainability Wedding Cake

One way to understand the SDGs is through the Sustainability Wedding Cake framework. It organizes the goals into three interdependent layers. Biosphere.

Society. Economy.

The logic is simple. Economic activity depends on social stability. Social stability depends on a functioning planet. If the base collapses, everything above it does too.

The Biosphere Layer
The foundation of the wedding cake is the biosphere. These goals protect the systems that make life and development possible.

SDG 6 Clean Water and Sanitation focuses on access to safe water and sanitation. Without it, health systems fail, and ecosystems degrade.

SDG 13 Climate Action addresses emissions, resilience, and adaptation. Climate instability amplifies every other risk.

SDG 14 Life Below Water protects oceans that regulate climate and feed billions.

SDG 15 Life on Land addresses deforestation, biodiversity loss, and soil degradation.

These goals are non-negotiable. They are preconditions, not preferences.

The Society Layer
Built on the biosphere is society. This layer focuses on human well-being, inclusion, and institutional strength.

SDG 1 No Poverty and SDG 2 Zero Hunger address basic survival and dignity.

SDG 3 Good Health and Well Being recognizes that development without health is hollow.

SDG 4 Quality Education creates the capacity to adapt and innovate.

SDG 5 Gender Equality expands participation and opportunity.

SDG 7 Affordable and Clean Energy links social equity with environmental transition.

SDG 11 Sustainable Cities and Communities reflects the reality that most of the world now lives in urban areas.

SDG 16 Peace, Justice, and Strong Institutions anchors the entire system in trust, rule of law, and accountability.

Societies fail when these conditions erode, even if economic indicators look strong.

The Economy Layer
At the top sits the economy.

SDG 8 Decent Work and Economic Growth focuses on livelihoods and safety.

SDG 9 Industry, Innovation, and Infrastructure supports productivity and resilience.

SDG 10 Reduced Inequalities addresses distribution, not just growth.

SDG 12 Responsible Consumption and Production limits waste and inefficiency.

Economic growth is necessary. It is not sufficient. Without the lower layers, it is unstable.

SDG 17 Partnerships for the Goals
SDG 17 binds the layers together. It recognizes that none of these goals can be achieved in isolation. Coordination across governments, firms, and communities is not optional.

Global Goals Meet Local Decisions
The SDGs are global. The tradeoffs are local.

Cities decide where housing goes. Utilities decide how energy is generated. Planning boards decide whose projects advance and whose stall. The SDGs set direction. Local institutions determine outcomes.

This is where governance matters.

ICLEI and the Role of Local Governments
ICLEI, Local Governments for Sustainability, works with more than 2,500 local governments worldwide. Its premise is straightforward. Global goals succeed or fail at the city level.

New York City used ICLEI tools to inventory emissions and track compliance with Local Law 97, aligning with SDG 13 Climate Action.

Cape Town relied on ICLEI support during its water crisis, advancing SDG 6 Clean Water and Sanitation through demand management and infrastructure investment.

Malmö integrated renewable energy and district heating, advancing SDG 7 Affordable and Clean Energy and SDG 13 Climate Action.

These were not abstract commitments. They were political decisions, budget choices, and governance tests.

Why Tradeoffs Matter

The SDGs do not eliminate tradeoffs. They expose them.

Every city faces constraints. Land. Capital. Time. Political will. The SDGs provide a shared language for prioritization. They do not remove responsibility from decision makers.

Sustainability fails when goals are treated as slogans. It succeeds when institutions accept that tradeoffs are unavoidable and accountability is required.

Global goals only matter when someone locally is willing to decide, explain, and own the consequences.

That is the work.

THE PARIS AGREEMENT AND THE LIMITS OF CONSENSUS

The Paris Agreement is one of the most ambitious experiments in global coordination ever attempted. It reflects a simple truth and a hard constraint at the same time. Climate change is a shared problem. Power, accountability, and enforcement are not.

Adopted at COP21 in 2015, the agreement set a clear collective objective: to limit global warming to well below 2 degrees Celsius above pre industrial levels, while pursuing efforts to hold the increase to 1.5 degrees. It did not dictate how countries must get there. Instead, it relied on a voluntary architecture built around trust, transparency, and repetition.

At the center of the agreement are Nationally Determined Contributions. Each country sets its own climate targets and policies based on national circumstances. These commitments are not legally enforceable. There are no penalties for missing them. The theory was that sunlight, peer pressure, and public accountability would do what treaties historically have struggled to achieve.

Transparency is the enforcement mechanism Paris chose. Countries must regularly report emissions and progress toward their commitments. These reports are reviewed internationally, creating a shared factual baseline. Every five years, a global stocktake assesses collective progress and exposes the gap between ambition and reality. The assumption is that exposure leads to pressure, and pressure leads to action.

Climate finance is the other pillar holding the agreement together. Developed nations committed to mobilizing one hundred billion dollars annually to support developing countries. This was not charity. It was recognition that responsibility and vulnerability are unevenly distributed. Countries that contributed least to cumulative emissions often face the highest risks. Without financing, adaptation and mitigation remain slogans rather than strategies.

Paris has changed behavior. Renewable energy deployment has accelerated. Net zero targets have proliferated. Corporations have begun aligning operations with science based targets. Cities, which account for a large share of global emissions, have moved faster than many national governments. Networks like C40 have shown how local leadership can translate global goals into operational plans.

But Paris also reveals the limits of consensus. Voluntary commitments move at the speed of politics. Financing pledges lag behind need. Fossil fuel dependence remains structurally embedded in many economies. Crises, whether financial, geopolitical, or public health related, routinely push climate action down the priority list.

The Paris Agreement does not fail because it lacks ambition. It strains because ambition without enforcement depends on governance, credibility, and follow through. It works best where institutions are strong, data is trusted, and accountability mechanisms exist. It falters where those conditions are weak.

Paris matters not because it solved climate change, but because it clarified the challenge. Global coordination is possible. Universal compliance is not guaranteed. Progress depends less on declarations than on whether countries, cities, firms, and investors translate shared goals into binding decisions.

The agreement is a framework, not a verdict. It tells us where the world says it wants to go. It does not tell us whether the systems of power, finance, and governance are strong enough to get us there.

WHY SMART PEOPLE DISAGREE, AND STILL HAVE TO DECIDE

One of the hardest truths about sustainability, policy, and development is this. Reasonable people, working with the same facts, often reach very different conclusions.

The Sustainable Development Goals make this tension visible. To some, they are a blueprint for shared progress. To others, they are a warning sign. Not because the goals themselves are hidden or secret, but because they sit at the intersection of power, trust, history, and implementation.

The disagreement is not accidental. It is structural.

Every SDG carries an intention and a fear. Ending poverty raises questions about redistribution. Food security triggers debates about technology and control. Public health invites concerns about surveillance and consent. Education sparks arguments over who decides what is taught. Climate action exposes fault lines around freedom, cost, and enforcement.

None of these concerns are inherently irrational. They emerge from past experiences, institutional failures, and uneven applications of policy. When people say they are worried about control, what they are often saying is that they do not trust the system to act fairly once authority is granted.

This is where many discussions go wrong. They treat skepticism as ignorance rather than as information.

The SDGs are not instructions. They are not laws. They do not tell governments or businesses how to act. They define outcomes the global community claims to value. What happens next depends entirely on governance, transparency, and accountability.

That distinction matters.

A goal to reduce inequality does not mandate uniformity. A goal to promote clean energy does not prescribe a single technology. A goal to build sustainable cities does not require surveillance or centralization. Those outcomes arise from choices made later, by institutions closer to power.

Which brings us to the uncomfortable part.

Disagreement does not absolve anyone from deciding.

Investors still allocate capital. Governments still write zoning codes. Developers still choose sites and materials. Cities still approve permits. Data still gets collected. Tradeoffs still get made. The absence of consensus does not pause the system.

Critical thinking, then, is not about choosing a side. It is about understanding where judgment enters the process and refusing to pretend it does not exist.

That means asking who defines success, who bears risk, who enforces compliance, and who has recourse when systems fail. It means separating goals from mechanisms and metrics from mandates. It means recognizing that transparency without accountability creates cynicism, while authority without trust creates resistance.

The SDGs surface disagreement because they force values into the open. That is not a flaw. It is a signal.

Smart people disagree because complex systems produce uneven outcomes. But they still have to decide, because cities get built anyway.

The real question is not whether disagreement exists. It is whether decisions are made honestly, visibly, and with consequences attached.

SECTION 3: ESG, CSR, AND MATERIALITY

ESG, CSR, AND THE PROBLEM OF PURPOSE

There is an old story about six blind men asked to describe an elephant. Each touches a different part and reaches a different conclusion. One feels a rope. Another a wall. Another a spear. All are describing the same animal. None is wrong. None is complete.

That is how ESG is usually discussed.

Lawyers see regulation. Engineers see energy. Planners see cities. Social advocates see equity. Investors see risk. Each perspective is valid. Each is partial. The confusion begins when people mistake their slice of the elephant for the whole.

This chapter is about purpose. What ESG is meant to do. What it is not meant to do. And why confusing ESG with values or decisions creates more heat than light.

What ESG Is and What It Is Not
ESG stands for Environmental, Social, and Governance. At its core, ESG is a reporting framework. It describes conditions. It captures exposure. It documents performance. It does not tell anyone what to do.

Full stop.

ESG does not embed judgment. It does not rank values. It does not resolve tradeoffs. It functions much like a medical report. The report shows cholesterol, blood pressure, and heart rate. It does not decide whether you should run more, eat fewer donuts, or change nothing at all. That decision belongs to the patient, the doctor, or the insurer. Not the report.

ESG emerged to make nonfinancial risks visible to capital markets. Environmental exposure. Workforce stability. Governance integrity. It gained prominence after the 2004 report Who Cares Wins, convened by the United Nations with global financial institutions. By the late 2000s, investors began treating ESG data as material to long-term performance. By 2023, more than thirty trillion dollars in assets referenced ESG data in some form.

That growth also exposed its limits. Data quality varies. Definitions differ. Reporting can be selective. ESG can be misused as marketing. But none of that changes its core function. ESG reports. People decide.

Frameworks like GRI and SASB exist to standardize disclosure, not to prescribe outcomes. When a company says it has an ESG strategy, what it should mean is that it measures its impacts consistently and transparently. Whether those measurements lead to action depends on governance, incentives, and values outside the framework.

The Role of Regulation

Regulation sets minimum standards. ESG sits alongside regulation, not above it.

Carbon limits, labor protections, data privacy laws, and governance requirements define what companies must do. ESG captures how companies perform within and beyond those boundaries. Firms may exceed regulatory requirements due to investor pressure, cost savings, reputation, or long-term risk management. That choice is strategic, not mandatory.

ESG emerged precisely because regulation alone proved insufficient. Environmental disasters, labor failures, and governance scandals exposed risks that were legal but not sustainable. ESG made those risks legible to investors. It did not solve them.

What CSR Tries to Do

Corporate Social Responsibility addresses a different problem. CSR is about intent. It reflects how companies choose to behave beyond compliance. It includes philanthropy, ethical sourcing, community investment, and workforce initiatives. CSR is voluntary by design.

Historically, CSR grew from charitable activity into broader stakeholder thinking. By the late twentieth century, globalization and environmental crises pushed CSR into the mainstream. Companies began publishing responsibility reports and aligning with frameworks like the UN Global Compact.

CSR can build trust. It can strengthen culture. It can improve reputation. It can also drift into symbolism. Without measurement, CSR risks becoming narrative without accountability.

Where ESG and CSR Diverge

CSR expresses values. ESG records performance.

CSR often emphasizes stories. ESG emphasizes data.

CSR asks what a company wants to stand for. ESG shows what a company is exposed to and how it behaves.

Problems arise when CSR claims are not supported by ESG data. Or when ESG data is published without governance structures that force action. Greenwashing thrives in that gap.

The two are most effective when aligned. CSR articulates purpose. ESG tracks whether behavior matches that purpose. Neither replaces judgment. Neither resolves tradeoffs. Both inform decisions that still have to be made by people with power.

The Problem of Purpose

The mistake is not using ESG. The mistake is asking it to do work it was never designed to do.

ESG will not tell cities how to grow. It will not tell developers what to build. It will not tell investors what values to prioritize. It will tell them what is happening, where risks sit, and where inconsistencies appear.

Purpose comes from governance. Accountability comes from institutions. Outcomes come from decisions.

Confusing reporting with responsibility does not eliminate conflict. It hides it.

And hidden tradeoffs do not disappear. They simply reemerge later, at a higher cost.

WHAT COUNTS, WHO DECIDES, AND WHO IT LEAVES OUT

Every sustainability conversation eventually runs into the same problem. You cannot measure everything. So someone has to decide what counts.

That decision is not technical. It is political, economic, and institutional.

Materiality is the mechanism we use to make that choice appear neutral.

At its simplest, materiality asks a practical question. What information matters enough to report? But beneath that question sits a more uncomfortable one. Who gets to define relevance, and whose concerns are ignored in the process?

Consider a college transcript. A biology major and a math major share general requirements, but their core courses diverge quickly. Two biology majors, however, will look far more similar. Sustainability reporting works the same way. There are metrics that matter across an industry, and others that only make sense within a specific sector. What is material for an office building may not be material for a data center, a multifamily portfolio, or a self-storage facility.

Good reporting distinguishes signal from noise. Bad reporting overwhelms with data while avoiding accountability.

The challenge is that sustainability reporting lacks the discipline of financial reporting. There is no single equivalent to GAAP or IFRS. That gap allows companies to disclose selectively, highlight strengths, and quietly omit weaknesses. The result is comparability without clarity and transparency without trust.

This is why materiality assessments matter.

Materiality and the Illusion of Neutrality

A materiality assessment is often presented as an objective exercise. In practice, it is a structured negotiation among stakeholders with unequal power.

Companies identify stakeholders, review industry trends, assess geographic and regulatory risks, and rank issues using tools like a materiality matrix. The process appears systematic. The outcomes reflect priorities.

When done well, materiality focuses attention on issues that genuinely shape performance and impact. When done poorly, it becomes a shield that explains away uncomfortable disclosures.

Transparency does not come from publishing more charts. It comes from explaining why certain issues were elevated and others were not. Accountability depends on that explanation.

Different Ways Issues Become Material

Not all materiality is the same. Different lenses produce different conclusions.

Financial materiality focuses inward. It asks how risks and opportunities affect financial performance and long term value. Rising energy costs, labor shortages, and insurance exposure are financially material because they directly shape operating outcomes.

Impact materiality looks outward. It considers how a company's actions affect communities, ecosystems, and society, regardless of immediate financial consequences. Energy use in data centers, plastics pollution, or displacement effects in housing may be materially significant even before they show up on an income statement.

These two perspectives increasingly overlap. This is known as dual materiality. Renewable energy investments can reduce operating costs while lowering emissions. Water conservation can cut expenses while protecting shared resources. In these cases, financial and social impacts converge.

There are also issues that become material through perception rather than balance sheets. Reputational materiality reflects how trust, brand value, and public confidence are shaped over time. Data breaches, labor practices, or safety failures may not immediately threaten profitability, but they erode legitimacy.

Materiality is also dynamic. Issues that appear marginal today can become decisive tomorrow as regulations change, technologies shift, or social expectations harden. Climate risk, biodiversity loss, and data privacy followed this path.

Finally, there is stakeholder materiality. Some issues matter deeply to specific groups even when they are not yet financially decisive. Workforce fairness, community engagement, and local impacts often fall into this category. Ignoring them can create long term instability that metrics fail to capture early.

From Materiality to Metrics

Once materiality is defined, metrics follow. This is where abstraction becomes operational.

Metrics generally fall into two categories. Universal metrics apply across sectors and enable broad comparison. Emissions, energy use, workforce composition, and governance practices sit here. They allow investors and regulators to see patterns across markets.

Sector specific metrics reflect how sustainability actually shows up in practice. Data centers track power and water intensity. Residential real estate tracks water use, tenant outcomes, and affordability pressures. Offices focus on energy performance and indoor conditions.

The danger lies in imbalance. Universal metrics without sector depth flatten reality. Sector metrics without common baselines make comparison impossible.

Frameworks like GRI and SASB attempt to structure this balance. They provide guidance, not mandates. That flexibility allows relevance but invites selectivity. One firm reports energy intensity. Another reports certifications. Both claim leadership. Neither may be fully comparable.

Standardization is not about perfection. It is about narrowing the space where omission can hide.

Why This Matters

Materiality determines visibility. Visibility shapes accountability. Accountability influences behavior.

When companies decide what to report, they are also deciding whose risks matter and whose concerns wait. That choice does not disappear because it is framed as technical.

Good sustainability reporting does not eliminate judgment. It makes judgment visible. And once judgment is visible, it can be questioned, compared, and improved.

REPORTING STANDARDS AND RATING TOOLS

Once organizations decide what counts, the next question follows immediately. How is it reported, compared, and judged?

This is where standards and rating tools enter the system. They do not create values. They translate performance into formats capital markets, regulators, and stakeholders can read. Understanding what each tool is designed to do is essential, because none of them serves the same purpose.

Confusing them is one of the most common sources of frustration in sustainability reporting.

GRI and the Logic of Transparency
The Global Reporting Initiative, founded in 1997, is the most widely used sustainability reporting framework in the world. GRI was built around a simple idea. Organizations should disclose their impacts on the economy, society, and the environment in a consistent and comparable way.

Over time, GRI evolved from environmental guidelines into a comprehensive framework covering social and governance topics. Its emphasis is not financial materiality alone, but impact. Who is affected, how, and at what scale.

GRI aligns closely with the Sustainable Development Goals and is designed for a broad stakeholder audience, including communities, employees, regulators, and civil society. It answers the question: what are the consequences of an organization's activities.

SASB and Financial Relevance
The Sustainability Accounting Standards Board took a different approach. Founded in 2011, SASB focused on financial materiality. Its standards are industry-specific and designed to integrate with financial reporting systems like GAAP and IFRS.

SASB asks a narrower question than GRI. Which environmental, social, and governance issues are likely to affect financial performance in a given industry? For real estate, that might include energy use intensity, climate exposure, or tenant concentration. SASB does not attempt to capture everything that matters socially. It captures what is likely to matter financially.

SASB's merger into the Value Reporting Foundation and subsequent consolidation under the International Sustainability Standards Board reflects a broader effort to align sustainability disclosure with capital markets.

Climate Disclosure and Risk

Some frameworks exist to surface specific categories of risk. The Carbon Disclosure Project focuses on environmental transparency related to climate change, water security, and deforestation. Its scoring system evaluates how organizations measure, manage, and lead on these issues.

The Task Force on Climate-related Financial Disclosures approaches the problem differently. Established by the Financial Stability Board, TCFD frames climate change as a financial risk. It asks organizations to disclose governance, strategy, risk management, and metrics related to climate exposure.

Physical risks such as extreme weather and transition risks such as policy shifts are central to this framework. TCFD does not prescribe climate action. It forces organizations to show whether they understand their exposure.

From Voluntary Frameworks to Regulation

As sustainability reporting matured, voluntary frameworks began to intersect with regulation.

The Federal Trade Commission's Green Guides exist to police how environmental claims are made. They do not measure sustainability performance. They prevent misleading statements.

The International Sustainability Standards Board represents a more significant shift. Established by the IFRS Foundation, the ISSB aims to create a global baseline for sustainability related financial disclosure. Its focus is consistency and comparability for investors.

In Europe, the Corporate Sustainability Reporting Directive goes further. It mandates detailed ESG disclosure, third party assurance, and double materiality. What affects the firm and what the firm affects. The CSRD signals a move from optional transparency to enforced accountability.

Ratings, Scores, and Market Interpretation

Once data is disclosed, rating agencies translate it into signals investors can use.

MSCI, Sustainalytics, and Moody's ESG Solutions all provide analytics that link ESG factors to risk, creditworthiness, and portfolio construction. Each uses its own methodology. Each applies judgment in weighting issues. None claims to offer an objective truth.

Ratings simplify complexity. They make comparison possible. They also introduce disagreement. Different ratings for the same company are not a flaw. They reflect different assumptions about what matters.

In real estate, GRESB plays a similar role at the portfolio and firm level. It benchmarks performance across energy, water, carbon, governance, and resilience. It does not certify sustainability. It compares disclosed performance.

Measuring Emissions and Setting Targets

Some tools focus narrowly on measurement. The Greenhouse Gas Protocol (GHG) defines how emissions are counted across Scope 1, Scope 2, and Scope 3. It provides a common language for carbon accounting.

Others focus on ambition. The Science-Based Targets initiative (SBTi) helps organizations align emissions reductions with climate science. The UN Principles for Responsible Investment (UNPRI) guide how capital allocators incorporate ESG considerations into investment processes.

Each tool serves a different function. Measurement. Disclosure. Benchmarking. Risk assessment. Commitment.

What These Tools Do and Do Not Do

None of these frameworks makes decisions. They surface information. They standardize language. They expose gaps.

They do not resolve tradeoffs between profit and impact. They do not determine acceptable risk. They do not replace governance.

The problem is not that there are too many tools. The problem is expecting tools designed to report performance to also define purpose.

Once reporting is confused with responsibility, accountability weakens.

Used correctly, these standards do exactly what they are meant to do. They make behavior visible. What happens next is still a choice.

And choices, not frameworks, shape outcomes.

OFFICE SECTOR MATERIALITY

The office sector exposes one of the central problems in sustainability reporting. Everyone agrees transparency matters. No one agrees on what should be disclosed.

When the Global Sustainability Standards Board launched the GRI Sector Program, it acknowledged that high-impact sectors required tailored standards. Mining and agriculture moved first. Real estate did not. Offices, despite their scale and visibility, were left to improvise.

The result has been predictable. Fragmented disclosures. Selective metrics. CSR reports heavy on narrative and light on comparability. Plenty of claims. Very little accountability.

GRI continues to work toward sector guidance for real estate. SASB offers flexibility but little enforcement. In the absence of consensus, firms choose what to highlight and what to omit. That is not a failure of intent. It is a failure of structure.

If sustainability reporting is meant to inform decisions, the office sector needs a clearer frame.

While this chapter uses the office sector as an illustrative case, the logic does not stop there. Every real estate asset class faces the same problem of selective disclosure and weak comparability. Residential, data centers, telecom, timberland, self-storage, and gaming each require sector-specific metrics layered on top of universal disclosures. My related research develops and tests these metrics across multiple property types, but the purpose here is not to catalog them. It is to show how structure changes behavior.

Separating Purpose From Performance
One way forward is to separate reporting by audience and function.

CSR speaks to employees, tenants, and communities. ESG speaks to investors, lenders, and analysts. Mixing the two clouds both.

A unified report can hold both, but only if the distinction is explicit. CSR explains commitments and culture. ESG discloses exposure, performance, and risk. When everything is blended together, nothing can be evaluated cleanly.

Using offices as an example, the logic becomes clear.

Universal Metrics Set the Floor
Some metrics should apply across real estate regardless of asset type.

On the environmental side, this includes greenhouse gas emissions, energy consumption by source, water use, and waste diversion. These metrics allow basic comparison across portfolios and markets. They reveal scale and trend. They show direction, not intent.

Social metrics focus on people who operate, occupy, and are affected by buildings. Workforce engagement, tenant satisfaction, diversity in leadership, and community investment belong here. These metrics make the human impact of office assets visible.

Governance metrics show whether transparency and accountability exist. Compliance with disclosure laws, board composition, executive pay ratios, ethics violations, and cybersecurity readiness indicate how decisions are made and enforced.

Resilience is not a separate category. It cuts across environmental, social, and governance decisions. Investment in risk mitigation, completion of climate and operational risk assessments, insurance outcomes, and continuity planning show whether firms are preparing for disruption or assuming stability will hold.

These metrics form a baseline. They do not explain how offices function. They establish comparability.

Sector Specific Metrics Reveal Reality
Office buildings operate in ways that differ from other real estate assets. Sector-specific metrics must capture that reality.

Environmentally, offices are measured at the building level. Energy and water use intensity. Indoor air quality. Renewable energy adoption. Certification status. Proximity to transit. Support for low-carbon commuting. These metrics connect sustainability claims to physical performance.

Socially, offices succeed or fail based on occupant experience. Access to daylight.

Wellness amenities. Accessibility compliance. Health certifications. Tenant turnover. Education and engagement programs. These measures show whether buildings support productivity and well-being or simply meet minimum code.

Governance at the asset level is about execution. Inspection outcomes. Regulatory violations. Tenant rights compliance. Data protection practices. Disclosure accuracy. These metrics indicate whether systems work in practice, not just on paper.

Resilience is not a separate category. It is revealed through environmental exposure, social stability, and governance discipline. Climate exposure, smart building capability, occupancy stability, investment in upgrades, and disaster recovery planning show whether an office asset can absorb shocks without cascading failure.

Collected at the building level, these metrics expose strengths and weaknesses. Aggregated at the portfolio level, they reveal strategy.

Why This Matters

Office buildings sit at the intersection of energy use, work patterns, urban form, and capital markets. What gets measured shapes how they evolve.

When reporting is vague, performance drifts. When metrics are selective, trust erodes. When standards are clear, behavior changes.

Materiality is not about perfection. It is about visibility.

The office sector does not need more storytelling. It needs clearer signals about what counts, who decides, and what happens when performance falls short.

That is how reporting becomes accountability.

WHAT THE FREE MARKET SOLVES, AND WHAT IT DOES NOT

At some point in every sustainability discussion, someone asks the obvious question. If markets are so good at allocating resources, why not let them handle this too?

It is a fair question. Markets are extraordinary tools. They reward efficiency, punish waste, and surface innovation faster than most institutions ever could. Much of modern prosperity exists because markets were allowed to work.

But markets do not solve every problem. And pretending they do creates its own risks.

The free market is not a moral system. It is an incentive system. It responds to prices, signals, and constraints. When something is not priced, not visible, or not enforced, markets treat it as if it does not matter.

That is not a failure of capitalism. It is a description of how it works.

Externalities Are Invisible Until Someone Prices Them

Markets struggle with costs that fall outside the transaction. Pollution, public health impacts, infrastructure strain, and climate risk are classic examples. When a firm can shift costs onto the public, the market rewards that behavior.

Left alone, markets do not correct this. They optimize around it.

Rules, taxes, standards, and disclosure requirements exist to bring those external costs back into view. They do not replace markets. They make markets work better by aligning private incentives with public consequences.

Choice Alone Does Not Scale

Consumer preference matters. But it does not reliably solve collective action problems.

Most people want clean air, safe buildings, and fair labor practices. They also want affordable prices. In competitive markets, firms that move first often pay the cost while competitors free ride.

Markets can reward sustainability eventually. They rarely do it quickly or evenly.

That is why baseline standards matter. They prevent a race to the bottom and allow innovation to happen on a level field.

Short Horizons Dominate Long Systems

Markets are excellent at optimizing near-term returns. Cities, infrastructure, and buildings operate on decades.

When payoffs are long dated and risks are diffuse, markets underinvest. Climate resilience, workforce development, and public infrastructure fall into this category.

Governance exists to stretch the time horizon. Not to eliminate profit, but to prevent short term optimization from undermining long term stability.

Power Is Not Evenly Distributed

Markets do not operate among equals. Size, access to capital, political influence, and information asymmetry matter.

Left unchecked, markets concentrate advantage. Smaller firms, tenants, and communities often absorb downside risk while upside accrues elsewhere.

This is where rules matter most. Not to micromanage outcomes, but to protect basic fairness and access.

The Role of Business Is Broader Than Price

Businesses do not operate in isolation. They depend on labor, infrastructure, trust, and legitimacy.

Firms that ignore workforce stability, data protection, or community impact may succeed briefly. Over time, those risks surface as turnover, regulation, litigation, or reputational loss.

Markets eventually respond. They are rarely early.

Why ESG Exists

ESG does not replace markets. It supplies information markets were missing. Disclosure makes risk visible. Standards make comparison possible. Governance determines whether information leads to action.

In that sense, ESG is not a constraint on markets. It is a correction to incomplete signals.

Free markets remain essential. They drive innovation, efficiency, and growth. But they operate inside systems. Those systems determine whether value creation is durable or extractive.

Markets decide many things well. They do not decide what is acceptable.

That judgment belongs elsewhere.

SECTION 4: THE SOCIAL CONTRACT

PEOPLE ARE NOT EXTERNALITIES

ESG organizes disclosure. This section examines what those disclosures often fail to explain: how social outcomes are produced, and who is accountable when they are not.

People experience the consequences of real estate decisions long before spreadsheets do.

When buildings are planned, financed, and managed, the effects ripple outward. Who gets to live there. Who gets displaced. Who works there. Who benefits. Who absorbs risk. These outcomes are not accidental. They are the result of choices.

What is often labeled the "social" dimension of ESG exists to make those choices visible. Not as sentiment, but as consequence.

At its core, this section asks whether value is being created by ignoring people or with them. It focuses on fairness, access, safety, dignity, and opportunity across employees, tenants, suppliers, and communities.

In real estate, this is not abstract. Buildings shape daily life. They determine access to housing, jobs, transportation, health, and stability. Social outcomes are not side effects of development. They are products of it.

What This Section Actually Covers

This section examines how organizations treat people across the full real estate value chain. That includes labor practices, workplace safety, wages, benefits, and workforce development. It includes supply chain accountability, ensuring that goods and services are not produced through exploitation or abuse.

It includes community engagement, not as a public relations exercise, but as a risk and legitimacy issue. Projects that ignore community impact rarely fail quietly. It includes tenant rights, customer safety, and data protection as buildings become increasingly digital.

In real estate, social performance shows up in affordability, displacement, access to transit, indoor air quality, accessibility, and neighborhood stability. These are not soft issues. They determine whether projects are accepted, resisted, regulated, or litigated.

Shareholders, Stakeholders, and the Shift in Responsibility

For much of the twentieth century, corporate responsibility was framed narrowly. Maximize shareholder returns. Everything else was secondary unless required by law.

That logic treated social and environmental impacts as external to the firm.

Stakeholder theory rejects that assumption. It recognizes that employees, tenants, suppliers, communities, and institutions all bear risk and create value. When those groups are ignored, the costs do not disappear. They surface later as turnover, opposition, regulation, or reputational damage.

This shift does not ask companies to abandon profitability. It asks whether profits are being generated by transferring risk onto people who have no voice in the transaction.

The History the Industry Cannot Avoid

Real estate cannot separate itself from the history of housing discrimination in the United States.

Redlining was institutional. Federal policies in the 1930s systematically denied mortgage access to Black and minority neighborhoods, cutting entire communities off from homeownership and wealth building.

Restrictive covenants reinforced segregation by law. Urban renewal displaced communities under the banner of progress. Eminent domain was often used to remove people with the least political power.

Bruce's Beach, where a thriving Black-owned beach resort was seized by local authorities in the 1920s, is not an anomaly. It is an example.

The result is a durable racial wealth gap and spatial inequality that persists today. Many formerly redlined neighborhoods still face lower investment, lower valuations, and higher vulnerability.

Ignoring that history does not make it irrelevant. It makes new projects more likely to repeat it.

Why Real Estate Is Different

Real estate operates at the intersection of land, capital, and policy. That creates leverage. It also creates responsibility.

Developers and owners influence who stays, who leaves, and who gains access. Decisions about affordability, financing, tenant protections, and community engagement shape outcomes for decades.

Responsibility in real estate is not charity. It is risk management and legitimacy.

Affordable housing reduces volatility. Community engagement reduces opposition. Fair lending expands markets. Workforce development stabilizes operations. Inclusive planning strengthens long-term demand.

These are not moral arguments. They are structural ones.

Why This Still Matters

Projects that ignore social consequences often move faster at first and stall later. Projects that account for people early face fewer disruptions and build durable support.

Firms that invest in fair labor practices, safety, and development retain talent. Firms that protect tenant rights and data earn trust. Firms that engage communities reduce entitlement risk.

Investors benefit as well. Socially resilient assets tend to be more stable across cycles. They face fewer shocks, fewer conflicts, and fewer surprises.

Residents experience the difference directly. Access to stable housing, transportation, services, and opportunity determines whether neighborhoods thrive or fracture.

This section insists on a basic truth.

People are not externalities. They are the system.

THE POLICIES THAT SHAPED WHERE PEOPLE COULD LIVE

Where people live in the United States has never been accidental. It has been shaped by law, policy, and power, often long before markets ever entered the picture.

The foundations of American social policy were laid through a series of decisions about freedom, citizenship, labor, and access. These decisions determined who could own property, who could vote, who could work under fair conditions, and who could be excluded by design. Housing outcomes followed.

Early reforms addressed fundamental injustices. The abolitionist movement challenged the moral and economic foundations of slavery. Leaders like Frederick Douglass and Harriet Tubman forced the country to confront the contradiction between liberty and bondage. The women's rights movement, formalized at the Seneca Falls Convention in 1848, challenged legal and economic exclusion. Education reformers like Horace Mann argued that public education was essential to democracy, while Dorothea Dix pushed the nation to recognize humane mental health care as a public responsibility.

These movements established a principle that would echo through housing and land use policy. Government action could expand opportunity or restrict it. Often both.

Lincoln & Johnson
The presidencies of Abraham Lincoln and Andrew Johnson marked a turning point. The Thirteenth Amendment abolished slavery in 1865, redefining citizenship and labor in the United States. The Freedmen's Bureau followed, providing education, housing assistance, and employment support to formerly enslaved people. For the first time, the federal government asserted a direct role in social welfare and economic inclusion.

After Lincoln's assassination, Andrew Johnson presided over Reconstruction with far less commitment to racial equality. While the Freedmen's Bureau continued, Johnson's leniency toward former Confederate states and resistance to civil rights protections weakened enforcement. The result was a fragile transition where formal freedom existed alongside rising exclusion. The lesson was clear. Rights without enforcement do not hold.

Grant, Hayes, and Garfield

Ulysses S. Grant attempted to strengthen Reconstruction. The Fifteenth Amendment protected voting rights regardless of race. The Enforcement Acts targeted violent suppression by the Ku Klux Klan. Federal troops were used to uphold civil rights, signaling that access and protection required federal authority.

At the same time, labor movements emerged. The Knights of Labor reflected growing demands for fair wages and safe working conditions. Economic inclusion was becoming inseparable from political rights.

That trajectory reversed under Rutherford B. Hayes. The Compromise of 1877 ended Reconstruction and withdrew federal troops from the South. Jim Crow laws followed. Segregation hardened. Housing access and economic mobility narrowed along racial lines.

James A. Garfield's presidency was brief, but consequential. His assassination exposed the corruption of the spoils system. The Pendleton Civil Service Reform Act, passed under Chester A. Arthur, introduced merit-based government employment. This reduced patronage and expanded access to stable public sector jobs. While not housing policy on its face, it shaped income stability and mobility, which directly affect where people can live.

Cleveland and Harrison

Grover Cleveland's first term reflected the growing tension between labor and capital. The Haymarket Riot underscored worker frustration with industrial conditions. The Interstate Commerce Act introduced federal regulation of railroads, acknowledging that unregulated markets could distort access and opportunity.

At the same time, the Dawes Act attempted to assimilate Native Americans by dividing tribal lands. The result was widespread land loss and cultural destruction. Property ownership was expanded for some by stripping it from others.

Benjamin Harrison advanced education and antitrust policy. The expansion of the Morrill Act supported land-grant colleges, including historically Black institutions. The Sherman Antitrust Act targeted monopolies, though enforcement remained weak. Efforts to protect voting rights stalled in Congress, revealing the limits of reform without political alignment.

Cleveland's second term saw renewed labor conflict. The Pullman Strike of 1894 ended with federal troops deployed against workers. The Supreme Court's decision in Plessy v. Ferguson soon followed, legalizing segregation under the doctrine of separate but equal. This ruling institutionalized spatial inequality for generations.

Why This History Matters

These policies shaped access to land, capital, and mobility. They determined which neighborhoods received investment and which were starved of it. They established patterns of inclusion and exclusion that continue to define housing markets today.

Social outcomes in real estate did not emerge organically. They were designed. Ignoring that history does not make current development neutral. It makes it blind.

Understanding where people could live requires understanding who decided, under what rules, and for whose benefit. That question remains unresolved.

GOOD INTENTIONS, REAL CONSEQUENCES

American social policy is often remembered for its intentions. Less often for its consequences.

From the Progressive Era onward, reforms sought to correct the abuses of industrial capitalism, expand rights, and improve public welfare. Many succeeded. Many also produced unintended effects that reshaped cities, housing markets, and access to opportunity in ways that still define real estate outcomes today.

Understanding this history requires holding two truths at once. Reform can expand opportunity. Reform can also concentrate risk, displace communities, and redraw the geography of advantage.

McKinley, Roosevelt, and Taft
William McKinley presided over rapid industrial expansion. The Gold Standard Act of 1900 stabilized currency and capital markets, reinforcing business confidence and industrial growth. Labor protections remained weak. Urban workers absorbed the costs through unsafe conditions and low wages. Housing followed employment, clustering workers near factories in overcrowded and underserved neighborhoods.

Theodore Roosevelt expanded the federal role in regulating markets. The Pure Food and Drug Act of 1906 established consumer protection and public health standards. The Antiquities Act asserted federal authority over land conservation. These reforms strengthened public trust, while also reinforcing the idea that government could shape land use and resource access.

William Howard Taft extended reform into child welfare and social protection. The creation of the Children's Bureau in 1912 marked a federal commitment to family stability and child labor reform. The Mann Act reflected growing concern over exploitation and mobility. Together, these policies influenced how families worked, moved, and settled within cities.

Wilson, Harding, and Coolidge
Woodrow Wilson expanded political inclusion through the Nineteenth

Amendment, reshaping civic participation and labor markets. His support for the Keating Owen Child Labor Act signaled recognition that unregulated labor markets imposed social costs, even though the law was later overturned.

Warren G. Harding focused on public health and veterans' welfare. The Sheppard Towner Maternity and Infancy Act introduced federal funding for maternal and child care, stabilizing households during economic transition. The Veterans Bureau expanded access to healthcare and benefits, reinforcing housing stability for returning soldiers.

Calvin Coolidge extended citizenship through the Indian Citizenship Act, while simultaneously enforcing Prohibition. These policies reshaped policing, land use, and community stability, particularly in urban and tribal areas.

Hoover, Roosevelt, and Truman

Herbert Hoover confronted the Great Depression through institutional intervention rather than direct aid. The Reconstruction Finance Corporation stabilized banks and municipalities. The Federal Home Loan Bank Act formalized federal involvement in mortgage finance, marking a turning point in housing policy.

Franklin D. Roosevelt dramatically expanded that role. The New Deal reshaped labor, income security, and housing finance. The Fair Labor Standards Act established minimum wages and working hour protections. The Social Security Act reduced income volatility across the life cycle. Federal housing programs standardized mortgage terms and expanded homeownership, while embedding racial and spatial exclusion through underwriting practices.

Harry Truman advanced civil rights and housing simultaneously. Executive Order 9981 desegregated the military. The Housing Act of 1949 funded public housing and urban redevelopment, expanding access while also accelerating displacement through urban renewal. Inclusion and removal often moved together.

Eisenhower, Kennedy, and Johnson

Dwight Eisenhower enforced civil rights protections through the Civil Rights Acts of 1957 and 1960. At the same time, the Federal Aid Highway Act reshaped metropolitan America. Highways connected regions and fueled suburban growth, while cutting through urban neighborhoods and displacing communities with limited political power.

John F. Kennedy advanced wage equity through the Equal Pay Act of 1963 and laid the groundwork for civil rights reform. His administration recognized that economic access and social inclusion were inseparable.

Lyndon B. Johnson's Great Society marked the most expansive social reform effort in U.S. history. The Civil Rights Act of 1964 and Voting Rights Act of 1965 dismantled legal segregation and expanded political power. Medicare and Medicaid reshaped access to healthcare. Education and anti poverty programs expanded opportunity. These reforms improved lives while interacting with zoning, finance, and infrastructure in ways that deepened spatial inequality.

Nixon, Ford, and Carter

Richard Nixon expanded environmental and social regulation. The creation of the Environmental Protection Agency linked environmental exposure to public health. Title IX transformed access to education and employment. Supplemental Security Income consolidated support for vulnerable populations, influencing where people could live safely and affordably.

Gerald Ford advanced disability rights and income support. The Education for All Handicapped Children Act reshaped access to schools and public space. The Earned Income Tax Credit supplemented wages, improving housing stability for working families.

Jimmy Carter elevated education and housing policy. The Housing and Community Development Act expanded federal investment in urban communities. Affirmative action policies strengthened access to opportunity. These efforts reflected recognition that markets alone could not correct inherited inequality.

Reagan, Bush, and Clinton

Ronald Reagan reduced the federal role in welfare and housing. Cuts to public housing and social programs shifted responsibility to states and households. The War on Drugs increased incarceration, destabilizing communities and housing markets.

George H. W. Bush signed the Americans with Disabilities Act, reshaping accessibility in buildings, workplaces, and public space. Clean Air Act amendments linked environmental quality to urban health outcomes.

Bill Clinton combined social investment with fiscal restraint. The Family and Medical Leave Act expanded worker stability. Welfare reform through PRWORA imposed limits and work requirements, reshaping income security. The Children's Health Insurance Program expanded healthcare access, reinforcing family stability.

Bush, Obama, Trump, and Biden
George W. Bush expanded healthcare access through Medicare Part D and reshaped education accountability through No Child Left Behind. Faith-based initiatives shifted service delivery to local institutions, affecting community-scale intervention.

Barack Obama expanded healthcare access through the Affordable Care Act and advanced civil rights protections. These reforms stabilized households and reshaped labor mobility.

Donald Trump enacted criminal justice reform through the First Step Act while reducing regulatory oversight. Housing and healthcare policy became more state-driven.

Joe Biden expanded federal involvement again through the American Rescue Plan, infrastructure investment, and healthcare reform. Broadband, transportation, and housing affordability returned to the center of economic policy.

Why This Matters
Every reform carried consequences. Some expanded access. Some concentrated risk. Many did both.

Housing outcomes reflect this history. Where people live today is the cumulative result of policies layered over time. Markets responded, but they did not decide alone.

Good intentions matter. So do outcomes.

Real estate sits at the intersection of both.

SOCIALLY RESPONSIBLE INVESTING IN REAL ESTATE

For most of modern history, investment decisions have been justified by one standard: financial return relative to risk. Everything else was considered secondary. Politics. Morality. Human consequence. These were treated as personal concerns, not investment criteria.

That assumption did not survive apartheid.

Apartheid was not an abstraction. It was a legally enforced system of racial separation that governed where people could live, work, travel, and own property in South Africa from 1948 until the early 1990s. Grand apartheid structured housing, employment, and land access by race. Petty apartheid enforced segregation in daily life.

The legal architecture made the intent unmistakable. The Prohibition of Mixed Marriages Act and the Immorality Amendment Act criminalized interracial relationships. The Population Registration Act classified every individual as Black, White, Colored, or Indian, determining access to housing, education, employment, and mobility. Classification was often arbitrary. Families were split by appearance. Entire neighborhoods were reorganized by law.

Between 1960 and 1983, more than three million Black South Africans were forcibly removed from their homes and relocated to segregated areas. Real estate was not collateral damage. It was the mechanism.

When Capital Was Forced to Choose

By the 1970s, pressure began to shift from governments to corporations.

Reverend Leon Sullivan, a board member of General Motors, proposed the Sullivan Principles in 1977. They called on U.S. companies operating in South Africa to oppose racial discrimination in employment and workplace practices. The logic was direct. If governments would not act, capital would.

The principles spread quickly. More than one hundred companies ultimately withdrew from South Africa during the disinvestment movement of the 1980s. Universities, pension funds, and institutional investors followed. For the first time, large pools of capital accepted that where money was invested could either reinforce or challenge an unjust system.

The U.S. government moved more slowly. Cold War politics treated South Africa as a strategic ally. That argument collapsed with the Sharpeville Massacre, mounting international pressure, and eventually the Comprehensive Anti Apartheid Act of 1986, which imposed economic sanctions.

Disinvestment did not end apartheid on its own. But it weakened the system. It raised costs. It removed legitimacy. It demonstrated that investment decisions could accelerate political and social change.

In 1999, Sullivan expanded the framework into the Global Sullivan Principles with the support of UN Secretary General Kofi Annan. Corporate responsibility was no longer framed as charity. It was framed as accountability.

Profit Alone, or Value Broadly Defined
Not everyone agreed.

Milton Friedman argued that the sole responsibility of business was to maximize shareholder value. Social objectives, in his view, belonged to governments and individuals, not corporations. Any diversion from profit was inefficiency. Any moral calculus inside the firm was a distortion of the market.

James Coleman disagreed from a different discipline. His work on social capital argued that economic outcomes depend on networks, trust, institutions, and relationships. Value is created not only through transactions, but through systems that allow people and markets to function.

This tension still defines real estate.

Is housing simply an asset class. Or is it infrastructure for human life.

From Externalities to Accounting
John Elkington reframed the debate in 1998 with the concept of the triple bottom line. People. Planet. Profit.

The idea was not that profit mattered less. It was that profit alone was an incomplete accounting system. Externalities did not disappear because balance sheets ignored them. They showed up elsewhere. In public health. In displacement. In environmental cleanup. In political backlash.

Real estate makes this visible faster than most industries. The cost of development decisions appears in neighborhoods long before it appears in quarterly reports.

Ethics, Performance, and Evidence
By the late 1990s, data began to challenge the assumption that ethical behavior reduced returns.

The Fortune 100 Best Companies to Work For list showed that firms investing in labor practices, culture, and governance consistently outperformed peers. Alex Edmans' research later confirmed that these companies generated superior long term stock performance.

Capital responded. Socially responsible investment products expanded. ESG screens entered institutional portfolios. Ethics stopped being treated as a constraint and started being treated as a signal.

Why This Matters for Real Estate
Real estate cannot pretend neutrality.

Property determines access to housing, jobs, education, transportation, and health. Investment decisions shape who stays, who leaves, and who bears risk. Displacement is not a market outcome alone. It is the result of capital choosing speed over legitimacy, yield over stability, extraction over durability.

Socially responsible investing in real estate is not about sacrificing returns. It is about understanding where returns come from and who pays for them.

The lesson from apartheid is not moral symbolism. It is structural clarity.

Capital is never neutral. Land is never abstract. And investment decisions always leave a footprint.

The question is whether that footprint reinforces exclusion or builds durable value.

PLACEMAKING, PLACEKEEPING, AND SOCIAL IMPACT ASSESSMENTS

Cities are not shaped only by capital and zoning. They are shaped by stories, memory, culture, and power. When development ignores those forces, places may look improved while communities unravel underneath.

That is where placemaking and placekeeping enter the conversation.

Creative placemaking emerged as a response to sterile redevelopment. It brings arts, culture, and public life into planning decisions. The goal is not decoration. It is activation. Public, private, philanthropic, and community actors collaborate to turn underused spaces into places where people gather, interact, and participate in civic life.

Placekeeping pushes further. It asks what happens after investment arrives. Who stays. Who leaves. What is preserved. It focuses on protecting the cultural, social, and historical identity of a community as change occurs. Placemaking can create energy. Placekeeping determines whether that energy displaces the people who generated it.

Together, they challenge a core assumption of development. That physical improvement automatically produces social benefit.

Public spaces designed through these lenses do more than function. They anchor identity. They support informal economies. They signal who belongs. When done well, they increase safety, pride, and resilience. When done poorly, they accelerate exclusion while claiming success.

The term creative placemaking was formalized by Ann Markusen and Anne Gadwa in 2010 for the National Endowment for the Arts. It gained traction because it delivered visible wins. Economic activity increased. Vacant areas became destinations. Cultural investment proved catalytic.

But success created its own risk. Cultural activation without protection often becomes a prelude to displacement. That is why placekeeping matters. Growth that erases identity is not revitalization. It is replacement.

Social Impact Assessments and Accountability
This is where Social Impact Assessments matter.

Social Impact Assessments, or SIAs, are designed to answer a question developers often avoid. Who is affected, and how.

SIAs evaluate both positive and negative outcomes of a project before decisions are locked in. They assess impacts on housing stability, access, employment, health, mobility, and social cohesion. They require stakeholder engagement, data collection, and scenario analysis. They force tradeoffs into the open.

Most importantly, they shift social outcomes from unintended consequences to measurable risks.

An effective SIA does not exist to approve a project. It exists to surface tension early. Mitigation strategies are developed before harm is irreversible. Monitoring continues after completion. Accountability does not end at ribbon-cutting.

When aligned with broader sustainability goals, SIAs help ensure projects generate value without externalizing costs onto communities least able to absorb them.

The High Line and the Cost of Success
The High Line illustrates both the promise and the limits of these tools.

Originally constructed in 1934 as part of the West Side Improvement, the elevated rail line removed dangerous freight trains from Manhattan streets. When rail traffic ended in 1980, the structure was abandoned. By the 1990s, demolition seemed inevitable.

Community advocates Robert Hammond and Joshua David proposed something else. Reuse rather than removal. They launched an ideas competition in 2003 and invited the public to imagine alternatives. Proposals ranged from a linear swimming pool to urban agriculture. The overwhelming response favored a public park.

The High Line became an international symbol of creative placemaking. It delivered green space, public art, tourism, and economic activity. Property values surged. New development followed.
It also became a case study in unmitigated success.

The same forces that made the High Line vibrant accelerated gentrification in surrounding neighborhoods. Long-term residents faced rising rents and displacement. Cultural activation preceded market pressure. Social benefits were real, but unevenly distributed.

The lesson is not that the High Line failed. It is that design alone cannot carry social responsibility. Without enforceable placekeeping strategies and rigorous impact assessment, even celebrated projects can transfer risk downward.

Designing for People, Not Just Places

Placemaking, placekeeping, and Social Impact Assessments are not aesthetic choices. They are governance tools.

They determine whether development builds legitimacy or resistance. Whether investment strengthens communities or fractures them. Whether public space signals inclusion or erasure.

Projects that engage communities early, protect cultural identity, and measure social outcomes move more slowly at first. They face fewer disruptions later. They trade speed for durability.

That is not sentiment. It is risk management.

Urban development will always change places. The question is whether it does so with the people who live there, or around them.

Placemaking creates opportunity. Placekeeping protects continuity. Social impact assessment enforces accountability.

Together, they determine whether growth becomes shared value or cascading failure.

AFFORDABLE HOUSING

Housing affordability is not a side issue. It is one of the clearest signals of whether a city is functioning or failing.

When housing costs rise faster than incomes, the consequences surface quickly. Workers move farther away. Commutes lengthen. Emissions rise. Families become unstable. Employers lose labor. Neighborhoods hollow out or harden along income lines. These are not abstract outcomes. They are structural ones.

Before addressing solutions, we need to be precise about how affordability is defined and who it is designed to serve.

How Affordability Is Measured

Area Median Income, or AMI, is the midpoint of household income in a given region. It is not an average. It is a sorting mechanism that determines eligibility for housing programs and financing structures.

Households earning below 30 percent of AMI are classified as extremely low income. Those between 30 and 50 percent are very low income. Low-income households fall between 50 and 80 percent of AMI. Moderate-income households earn between 80 and 120 percent. Above that threshold, housing is assumed to be market-supported.

These distinctions matter because they determine both subsidy design and risk exposure.

Households at the lowest income levels typically rely on direct public support such as housing vouchers. Moderate-income households often do not qualify for subsidies but still cannot afford market rents. This group includes teachers, healthcare workers, municipal employees, and first responders. Workforce housing exists to serve them, but supply rarely matches demand.

Fair Market Rent, or FMR, is the second critical benchmark. Calculated annually by HUD, FMR reflects the cost of modest housing, including utilities, in a specific market. It sets caps for voucher programs and anchors affordability assumptions to local conditions.

Together, AMI and FMR translate income distribution into housing outcomes. They are not neutral metrics. They shape who can live where.

What Affordable Housing Actually Means

Housing is considered affordable when total housing costs do not exceed 30 percent of gross household income. That standard is widely used because once housing consumes more than that share, tradeoffs become unavoidable. Healthcare is deferred. Education suffers. Savings disappear. Stability erodes.

Affordable housing spans multiple income bands. At the lowest levels, public subsidy covers most or all of the cost. As income rises, households are expected to contribute more, with subsidies tapering accordingly.

The objective is not dependency. It is continuity.

When workers can live near their jobs, communities function better. Commutes shorten. Labor markets stabilize. Carbon emissions decline. Schools retain students. Businesses retain employees. Housing affordability is not only a social concern. It is an economic and environmental one.

Delivering affordable housing requires coordination across policy, finance, and land use. Public-private partnerships combine public capital with private execution. Zoning reforms, density bonuses, and parking reductions make projects feasible. Tax credits, grants, and subsidized loans close funding gaps.

None of this works without discipline. AMI and FMR anchor affordability to reality. Without them, affordability becomes a slogan rather than a constraint.

Why Affordable Housing Matters

Affordable housing stabilizes communities by keeping residents anchored to place. Employers benefit from a reliable workforce. Local businesses gain customers. Municipal services operate more efficiently when displacement slows.

At the urban scale, affordable housing reduces sprawl and infrastructure strain. At the household scale, it improves health, educational outcomes, and financial resilience.

These are compounding effects. Cities that ignore affordability pay for it later through congestion, emissions, labor shortages, and political backlash.

Via Verde and Integrated Design

Via Verde in the South Bronx shows what is possible when affordability is treated as a system rather than a silo.

Completed in 2012, the project combines low-income rental housing, moderate-income cooperative ownership, healthcare services, and sustainability features in a single development. It was designed in response to specific local conditions, including high asthma rates and chronic health challenges.

The project includes 151 rental units for low-income households and 71 cooperative units for moderate-income residents, along with an on-site medical clinic. Community engagement shaped the design. Residents emphasized health, access to green space, and lower operating costs.

Those priorities translated into solar panels, green roofs, rainwater harvesting, energy-efficient appliances, and low-toxicity materials. The result was not only lower utility bills but improved public health outcomes.

The development team reflected the project's hybrid nature. A nonprofit developer ensured affordability and mission alignment. A for-profit partner brought capital discipline and long-term stewardship. Architects balanced functionality with dignity and design quality.

Financing was equally layered. Low Income Housing Tax Credits supported the rental units. The cooperative units were sold below market, creating a pathway to ownership. Healthcare services operated under a separate regulatory framework. Each component was structured independently, but the outcomes were shared.

That distinction matters. Integration does not require uniformity. It requires coordination.

Via Verde did not eliminate gentrification pressures in the surrounding neighborhood. No single project can. But it demonstrated that affordability, sustainability, and health can be designed together rather than traded off.

The Larger Lesson

Affordable housing is not charity. It is infrastructure.

Cities that treat it as optional discover that markets alone do not correct for displacement or exclusion. Cities that embed affordability into land use, finance, and design create more resilient systems.

The question is not whether affordable housing pays off. The question is when, and for whom.

Projects like Via Verde show that when affordability is treated as a core design constraint rather than an afterthought, the benefits extend far beyond the balance sheet.

That is not idealism. It is systems thinking.

SENIOR HOUSING

Senior housing is not a niche asset class. It is a demographic inevitability.

Across the United States and much of the developed world, populations are aging faster than housing systems are adapting. Longer life expectancy, declining birth rates, and rising housing costs have collided with a built environment designed for younger, more mobile households. The result is a growing mismatch between where people live and what they need to live well.

Senior housing exists to close that gap. At its best, it supports independence rather than dependency. At its worst, its absence pushes older adults into isolation, instability, or institutional care that could have been avoided.

The question is not whether senior housing is needed. It is whether it is designed as an integrated part of communities or treated as a segregated afterthought.

Designing for Aging, Not Decline
Effective senior housing begins with design choices that anticipate change rather than react to crisis.

Universal design principles allow residents to age in place. No step entries. Wider doorways. Accessible bathrooms. These are not aesthetic preferences. They are risk controls that reduce injuries, delay institutionalization, and lower long-term healthcare costs.

Location matters just as much as layout. Senior housing that is disconnected from transit, services, and social activity increases isolation. Housing that is embedded in walkable neighborhoods with access to healthcare, retail, and public space supports autonomy and dignity.

Programming matters too. Social activities, transportation options, and on-site or nearby medical services are not amenities. They are stabilizers. They reduce loneliness, improve mental health, and keep residents engaged with the life of the city.

Affordability remains the binding constraint. Fixed incomes do not rise with rents. Without subsidies, vouchers, or cross-subsidization within mixed-income developments, many seniors are priced out of the neighborhoods they helped build.

Why Senior Housing Strengthens Communities

Older residents are not a burden on communities. They are an asset.

They contribute institutional memory, cultural continuity, and informal social infrastructure. When seniors are displaced, neighborhoods lose stability. When they remain, communities retain depth.

Senior housing that is well designed does more than serve its residents. It reduces pressure on emergency healthcare systems. It supports caregivers. It stabilizes local economies. It creates environments where multiple generations can coexist rather than compete for space.

Cities that fail to plan for aging populations end up managing the consequences later through higher public costs and fragmented services.

Essex Crossing and Repairing Broken Promises

Essex Crossing on Manhattan's Lower East Side illustrates how senior housing can function as part of a broader effort to repair historical damage.

The site's history matters. In 1967, more than 1,800 low-income residents, many from Puerto Rican families, were displaced with promises of replacement housing that never materialized. For decades, the land symbolized neglect rather than renewal.

The redevelopment process that began in 2011 took a different approach. Community input shaped the plan. Affordable housing was not an accessory. It was central. Senior housing was included not as a standalone project, but as part of a mixed-use neighborhood.

The development spans six acres and includes residential units, retail, cultural institutions, and public space. Within its affordable housing allocation, dedicated senior units were designed to support aging in place. Accessibility features, proximity to services, and shared amenities allow older residents to remain active participants in neighborhood life.

Approval came in 2012. Construction began in 2015. Full completion is expected by 2024. The timeline matters because trust takes time to rebuild.

Outcomes That Matter

The senior housing component at Essex Crossing does more than provide shelter. It anchors older residents in a community that was once taken from them.

Accessible design reduces health risks. On-site and nearby amenities support daily living. Integration with a broader mixed-use environment reduces isolation. Seniors are not separated from families, workers, or cultural life. They are part of it.

This approach does not erase the harms of the past. But it acknowledges them. And it demonstrates that redevelopment can prioritize continuity rather than replacement.

The Larger Lesson

Senior housing works best when it is embedded, not isolated.

Treating aging as a housing problem rather than a medical one changes outcomes. Designing for independence rather than decline preserves dignity. Integrating seniors into mixed-use environments strengthens communities across generations.

As populations age, senior housing will become a defining test of whether cities are built for people across the full arc of life or only for those at their economic peak.

This is not about benevolence. It is about foresight.

Cities that plan for aging build resilience. Cities that ignore it inherit instability.

ACCESSIBLE HOUSING

Accessible housing is not a special category. It is a test of whether housing systems are designed for real people or idealized ones.

Disability is not rare. It is episodic, situational, and often temporary. Injury. Illness. Aging. Parenthood. Housing that only works for the fully mobile eventually fails most households. The question is not whether accessibility will be needed. It is when.

Accessible design begins with a simple premise. People should be able to live, move, and participate in daily life without unnecessary barriers. That premise has implications for how housing is designed, financed, regulated, and renovated.

Designing for Use, Not Exception

Accessible design works best when it is invisible. Universal design principles ensure that spaces are usable by everyone without signaling who they were built for. No step entries. Wider doorways. Clear circulation. Bathrooms and kitchens that work across a range of abilities.

Adaptable design goes further. It anticipates change. Features like reinforced walls for grab bars, flexible layouts, and accessible controls allow units to evolve with residents rather than forcing residents to move when circumstances change.

Technology now plays a central role. Automation, voice controls, lighting systems, and assistive devices allow residents to manage their environment independently. These tools are not luxuries. They are autonomy.

When accessibility is treated as an add-on, it becomes expensive and rare. When it is embedded in baseline design, it becomes scalable.

Policy, Incentives, and Accountability

Accessible housing does not appear on its own. It requires policy.

Civil rights legislation like the Americans with Disabilities Act established access as a right, not a favor. But enforcement alone is not enough. Zoning requirements, building codes, and financing rules determine whether accessible units are actually delivered.

Public subsidies, tax credits, and grants play a critical role, particularly in affordable housing and retrofits. Without them, developers often defer accessibility in favor of short-term cost savings. The result is higher long-term public expense through institutional care, emergency services, and displacement.

Accessible housing is not just a social outcome. It is a cost containment strategy.

Why Accessibility Changes Outcomes

Removing barriers changes behavior.

Residents who can navigate their homes and neighborhoods independently rely less on caregivers and institutions. Employment becomes more feasible. Social participation increases. Health outcomes improve.

For cities, accessible housing reduces pressure on hospitals, shelters, and long-term care facilities. For investors and operators, it stabilizes tenancy and reduces turnover driven by forced relocation.

Accessibility is not about accommodation. It is about keeping people housed.

Selis Manor and Designing With, Not For

Selis Manor in Manhattan's Chelsea neighborhood demonstrates what accessibility looks like when it is treated as a design problem rather than a compliance exercise.

Built in 1980, Selis Manor was the first government-funded residence in New York City designed specifically for visually impaired residents. The fourteen-story building includes 205 units supported through the Section 8 program and is managed by the New York City Housing Authority.

Over time, the building faced operational strain. A single shared entrance served residents and hundreds of daily visitors to VISIONS, a nonprofit providing services to the visually impaired. Congestion, security issues, and aging systems reduced livability.

In 2015, a 38-million-dollar rehabilitation project began. The goal was not only modernization, but usability.

Engagement as Design Infrastructure

What distinguished Selis Manor was how the project engaged residents.

Architect Chris Downey, who is visually impaired, played a central role in shaping the redesign. His lived experience informed decisions that conventional design reviews often miss.

Magnusson Architecture and Planning used tactile three-dimensional models to communicate proposed layouts. Residents could feel the space, understand circulation, and provide meaningful feedback. Design decisions were tested against daily use, not drawings alone.

Accessibility was treated as knowledge held by residents, not assumptions held by professionals.

Outcomes That Matter

The renovation delivered more than compliance.

A separate secure resident entrance improved safety. Apartments were upgraded with modern finishes and accessible layouts. Mechanical systems were replaced to improve energy efficiency. Terrazzo flooring with scored patterns and Braille inserts improved navigation.

Amenities like a roof terrace, fitness center, and auditorium expanded social space. Sustainability upgrades targeted certification under the NYSERDA Multifamily Participation Program, aligning accessibility with long term operating efficiency. Phased construction and temporary relocation minimized disruption. Residents were not displaced to make the project easier.

The Larger Lesson

Accessible housing works when it is designed into systems, not appended to them.

Designing with users produces better buildings. Policy aligned with lived reality produces better outcomes. Accessibility improves independence, stability, and resilience for individuals and communities alike.

Housing that only works for the able-bodied is fragile. Housing that anticipates difference is durable.

Accessible housing is not about serving a minority. It is about designing for the future most households will eventually reach.

WORKFORCE DEVELOPMENT

Buildings do not operate themselves. Every asset performs through people.

Workforce development is not a human resources function. It is an operational strategy. The quality, safety, and resilience of real estate assets depend on the skills, judgment, and stability of the people who design, build, operate, and maintain them.

Real estate is a labor-intensive industry. Property management, construction, compliance, facilities operations, and maintenance all require specialized and evolving skills. When those skills lag, risks rise. Accidents increase. Systems fail. Tenants notice.

Training is not optional. It is infrastructure.

Safety Is a Performance Variable
Safety failures are not random. They are predictable outcomes of insufficient training and weak accountability.

Construction and maintenance roles involve elevated risk. Falls, heat exposure, confined spaces, chemical handling, and equipment misuse remain leading causes of injury and death. OSHA data consistently shows that these incidents are preventable.

Job specific training matters. Fall protection, scaffolding protocols, ladder safety, and confined space procedures reduce fatalities when they are enforced and practiced. Heat management training is no longer seasonal. Rising temperatures have made hydration schedules, shaded rest areas, and heat illness recognition basic operating requirements.

Maintenance staff face different risks. Improper handling of cleaning agents and pest control chemicals exposes workers to long term health consequences. Training reduces exposure. It also reduces liability.

Organizations that invest in safety training experience fewer accidents, lower insurance costs, and more reliable operations. Safety is not a moral add-on. It is a cost and continuity issue.

Skills Keep Assets Relevant
The skill set required to operate real estate is changing.

Sustainability systems, smart building technologies, energy management platforms, and data-driven maintenance are now standard. Assets do not become intelligent on their own. People have to understand them.

Upskilling property managers, engineers, and operations staff allows buildings to perform as designed. Training in green building certifications, energy systems, and automation reduces operating inefficiencies and protects capital investments.

When staff lack these skills, owners pay twice. First through underperforming assets. Then through turnover and retraining.

Workforce development preserves asset value.

Workforce Stability Shapes Community Outcomes
Training affects more than internal operations. It shapes how projects interact with communities.

Skilled property managers resolve tenant issues faster. Clear communication reduces conflict. Well-trained maintenance teams prevent small problems from becoming visible failures.

Construction projects managed by trained, safety-conscious teams are less likely to experience delays, accidents, or shutdowns. Communities notice the difference. So do regulators.

Workforce development also influences who benefits from development. Hiring locally and training workers from surrounding neighborhoods strengthens legitimacy and reduces opposition. Projects that extract labor without building capacity tend to face resistance later.

Workforce training is a form of community engagement.

When Training Fails, Consequences Follow
The cost of neglect is visible.

In New York City, a construction worker fell from a fifteenth-floor scaffold due to inadequate fall protection. The result was a fatality, a stop-work order, and regulatory scrutiny. The failure was not technical. It was procedural.

In Houston, a temporary worker at Al Star Recycling LLC died from heat illness. OSHA found no heat management program and no training on heat stress prevention. The penalty followed the tragedy. The loss came first.

These incidents are not anomalies. They are warnings.

Accountability Is Increasing

Regulatory expectations are tightening.

New York's proposed Carlos' Law raises penalties for corporate negligence, setting minimum fines of hundreds of thousands of dollars for serious violations. The goal is deterrence through accountability.

OSHA's Severe Violator Enforcement Program targets repeat offenders and expands oversight. Training gaps are no longer treated as oversights. They are treated as failures of management.

Firms that invest in workforce development move ahead of enforcement rather than reacting to it.

Why Workforce Development Matters

Workforce development determines whether buildings are safe, adaptive, and trusted.

Organizations that train their people experience lower turnover, fewer disruptions, and stronger operational performance. Employees stay longer when they see pathways to growth and competence.

Investors benefit from reduced risk. Communities benefit from safer projects. Tenants benefit from responsive management.

Workforce development is not about compliance or culture statements. It is about whether the human systems inside buildings are as well designed as the physical ones.

Assets perform through people. Ignoring that reality is one of the most expensive mistakes real estate firms continue to make.

PRIVACY AND CYBERSECURITY

Real estate has become a data business, whether the industry admits it or not.

Smart buildings, tenant portals, IoT systems, digital leasing, and automated payments have quietly rewired how properties operate. These systems collect and store personal, financial, and behavioral data at scale. Tenant applications, rent payments, access logs, vendor contracts, building performance data. All of it now lives inside digital infrastructure that did not exist a generation ago.

That infrastructure creates value. It also creates exposure.

Privacy and cybersecurity are no longer technical back-office issues. They are governance issues. They determine whether tenants trust operators, whether regulators intervene, and whether assets remain functional when systems are attacked.

Why Real Estate is a Target

Real estate attracts cybercrime for three reasons.

First, the money is large and frequent. Rent flows, purchase deposits, refinancing transactions, and vendor payments move constantly across digital systems.

Second, the ecosystem is fragmented. Property managers, owners, lenders, brokers, law firms, contractors, and software vendors all touch the same data. Each connection is a vulnerability.

Third, much of the industry still runs on legacy systems layered with new technology. Old infrastructure was never designed to defend against modern threats.

Attack methods are well established. Ransomware locks property management systems and demands payment to restore access. Data breaches expose tenant financial and identity information. Phishing attacks exploit human behavior to steal credentials. IoT systems, from HVAC to access control, are hijacked to disrupt operations or gain network entry.

Data centers that support real estate operations are also targets. Without strong physical and digital security, they become single points of failure.

None of this is theoretical. It is already happening.

What Fails When Cybersecurity Fails

When cybersecurity fails, the damage spreads quickly.

Financial losses include regulatory fines, lawsuits, ransom payments, system restoration, and increased insurance costs. Operational disruptions delay rent collection, maintenance, leasing, and access control. Tenants lose confidence. Investors question management competence.

Reputational damage often lasts longer than the outage itself. Trust, once broken, is expensive to rebuild.

Cyber risk is not separate from asset risk. It is part of it.

Security Is an Operating Discipline

Effective cybersecurity is not a checklist. It is an operating discipline.

Encryption protects data in storage and transit. Access controls limit who can see and change sensitive information. These controls must apply not only to software platforms but also to data centers and physical infrastructure.

Regular backups allow recovery without paying ransom. Vendor due diligence matters because third-party platforms often introduce the weakest links. Penetration testing exposes vulnerabilities before attackers do.

Employee training is critical. Most breaches succeed because someone clicks the wrong link or trusts the wrong request. Technology alone does not solve that.

Cybersecurity investments do not eliminate risk. They reduce the blast radius when something goes wrong.

Privacy Is About Power, Not Policy

Privacy is not just about compliance with GDPR, CCPA, or disclosure notices.

It is about power.

Real estate firms increasingly know where people live, when they enter buildings, how they pay, and how they move through space. That information can be used responsibly or abused quietly.

Transparent data practices matter. Tenants should know what data is collected, why it is collected, and how it is used. Consent should be informed, not buried in fine print.

Algorithmic tools introduce new risks. Tenant screening systems can reinforce bias. Automated decisions can exclude without explanation. Fair data use requires oversight, not blind trust in software.

Privacy failures do not always show up as breaches. Sometimes they show up as discrimination, exclusion, or loss of dignity.

Lessons from Failure

The warning signs are visible.

A ransomware attack on Albyn Housing Society in Scotland exposed tenant and staff data after legacy systems were compromised.

In Connecticut, a homebuyer lost six hundred thousand dollars to wire fraud after hackers exploited weak email security in a real estate transaction.

These cases were not caused by sophisticated espionage. They were caused by predictable gaps in security and governance.

Why This Matters

Cybersecurity and privacy determine whether real estate remains operable under stress. They shape tenant trust, regulatory scrutiny, investor confidence, and operational resilience. Firms that treat them as technical details eventually pay for that assumption.

Technology will continue to reshape buildings and transactions. That shift is not reversible.

The question is not whether real estate will be digital. The question is whether the industry will govern its data with the same seriousness it applies to capital, safety, and physical risk.

Because when systems fail, buildings do not just go offline. People do.

SECTION 5: WHO DECIDES

WHO DECIDES AND WHO DOESN'T

Every real estate outcome begins with a governance choice.

Who sits at the table. What information counts. Which risks are acknowledged. Which voices are ignored. Governance is not paperwork. It is the system that decides whose interests are protected and whose are treated as collateral.

In real estate, those decisions shape cities, neighborhoods, and lives. They determine what gets built, who can afford to stay, how risk is allocated, and who absorbs failure when projects fall short.

Governance is the infrastructure behind every other outcome.

Governance Is About Power Before It Is About Process
Governance is often described as structure, compliance, and oversight. That language understates what is actually happening.

Governance decides how power moves through an organization. It determines who can approve capital, who can override concerns, and who is accountable when harm occurs. It links boards to management, management to operations, and operations to communities that rarely have a formal vote.

In real estate, governance connects financing decisions to land use, tenant protections, safety standards, and long term asset strategy. It determines whether sustainability is treated as a constraint, a marketing exercise, or a core risk discipline.

Strong governance does not eliminate conflict. It makes tradeoffs explicit and visible.

Whose Interests Are Protected
At its core, governance answers a simple question. Whose interests count when decisions are made.

For tenants and communities, governance shows up in fair housing practices, safety standards, data protection, and whether engagement is real or symbolic.

For employees, it determines whether labor standards, safety, and advancement are enforced or bypassed under pressure.

For investors and lenders, governance signals whether capital is deployed responsibly and whether risks are disclosed honestly. Transparent reporting, independent oversight, and clear accountability structures build confidence that returns are not being generated by hiding future liabilities.

Real estate operates inside dense regulatory environments. Zoning, building codes, housing law, environmental standards. Governance determines whether firms comply narrowly or treat regulation as a floor rather than a ceiling.

Reputation in this industry is not built by press releases. It is built by how firms behave when rules are inconvenient.

Governance as Risk Management
Governance is how organizations manage what they do not fully control.

Markets change. Climate risk intensifies. Social expectations shift. Technology introduces new exposure. Governance provides the mechanisms to adapt without improvising in crisis.

That includes internal controls, independent boards, audit functions, disclosure practices, and escalation pathways when something goes wrong. It also includes cultural norms that allow concerns to surface before they become liabilities.

Poor governance does not usually fail loudly at first. It fails quietly, through shortcuts, concentration of authority, and incentives that reward speed over scrutiny.

Proxy Voting and the Illusion of Voice
Proxy voting is one of the few formal tools investors have to influence governance.

In public markets, shareholders vote on board appointments, executive compensation, and shareholder proposals. In theory, this ensures accountability. In practice, power is often concentrated far from individual investors.

For those investing through large asset managers, proxy voting authority is delegated. That delegation matters.

Consider BlackRock. In 2021, it supported approximately forty three percent of environmental and social shareholder proposals. In 2022, support fell to roughly twenty-four percent. In 2023, support dropped to just seven percent, with the vast majority of proposals rejected.

BlackRock justified the shift by arguing that many proposals were overly prescriptive or misaligned with long-term shareholder value. Whether one agrees with that rationale is beside the point. The point is this. Governance power moved. And many investors did not realize it had.

Proxy voting reveals a central tension in modern governance. Participation exists, but influence is uneven. Values are expressed, but decisions are centralized.

Investors who assume their preferences are automatically reflected are often mistaken.

Governance Is Not Neutral

Governance frameworks are not neutral systems. They embed assumptions about value, risk, and responsibility.

They can amplify accountability or diffuse it. They can surface dissent or suppress it. They can align profit with long term stability or reward extraction while pushing costs outward.

Effective governance does not promise consensus. It promises visibility.

It makes clear who decides, how decisions are made, and who bears the consequences.

In real estate, that clarity matters because buildings outlast leadership cycles, market booms, and political administrations. The governance choices made today will shape outcomes for decades.

Governance is not about checking boxes. It is about deciding who gets a voice, who gets protection, and who gets left to absorb the fallout when decisions fail.

That is why governance matters. Not because it sounds responsible. But because it decides what responsibility actually means.

GOVERNANCE STRUCTURES

Governance structures are not organizational charts. They are decision machines.

They determine who has authority, how information flows, and what happens when incentives collide with long-term risk. In real estate, where capital is patient but consequences are permanent, governance structure often matters more than strategy.

The difference between a resilient organization and a fragile one is rarely vision. It is structure.

The Board, Committees, and Management

At the top of the governance system sits the board of directors. The board's role is not to manage day-to-day operations. It is to set direction, approve risk appetite, and hold leadership accountable when performance diverges from stated goals.

In real estate, boards oversee decisions that shape asset lifecycles, capital allocation, leverage, development strategy, and exposure to regulatory and community risk. A board that lacks independence, sector knowledge, or willingness to challenge management is not a safeguard. It is a rubber stamp.

Committees exist because no board can oversee everything at once. Audit committees focus on financial integrity and controls. Risk or sustainability committees focus on material exposures that do not show up cleanly in quarterly earnings. These committees matter only if they have authority, access to information, and direct lines to the full board.

Executive leadership translates governance into action. Management executes strategy, allocates resources, and responds to immediate pressures. This is where governance either holds or collapses. When leadership incentives are misaligned, even well-designed structures fail.

Checks and balances only work when friction is allowed. Speed without scrutiny is not efficiency. It is deferred risk.

Transparency Is a Governance Function
Transparency is not a communications strategy. It is a governance outcome.

Without clear disclosure, stakeholders cannot evaluate performance, assess risk, or hold leadership accountable. Transparency determines whether governance is real or cosmetic.

Reporting frameworks exist to impose discipline on disclosure. GRI emphasizes broad impacts across environmental, social, and governance dimensions. SASB focuses on financially material issues by sector. TCFD centers climate risk and financial resilience.

These frameworks do not create good governance. They reveal whether it exists.

Standardization is still evolving, but consistent reporting allows investors to compare firms, identify exposure, and distinguish between performance and narrative. Silence, inconsistency, or selective disclosure are governance signals, whether intended or not.

Transparency does not eliminate risk. It clarifies who is carrying it.

The Role of ESG Committees
ESG committees are only as effective as their mandate.

When empowered, they integrate sustainability into capital planning, operations, and risk management. When sidelined, they become reporting units disconnected from decision-making.

Effective ESG committees do three things. They track material risks and performance across the organization. They report directly to the board with clear metrics and escalation pathways. And they translate operational data into strategic insight.

They function as connectors. Between departments. Between metrics and decisions. Between long term exposure and short term pressure.

An ESG committee that cannot influence capital allocation or executive evaluation is not governing. It is documenting.

Executive Compensation Is Where Governance Becomes Real
Nothing reveals governance priorities more clearly than how leaders are paid.

Compensation structures signal what the organization actually values. When bonuses reward short term financial performance without regard to safety, social impact, or long term risk, governance has already failed.

Aligning executive compensation with measurable ESG outcomes changes behavior. It forces tradeoffs into the open. It makes sustainability a performance issue rather than a narrative one.

That alignment only works if metrics are material, verifiable, and tied to decision authority. Vague targets produce vague accountability.

Transparency in compensation matters as much as structure. Stakeholders want to know not just how much executives are paid, but why. Misalignment between pay and outcomes erodes trust quickly and visibly.

In real estate, where decisions create long-lived assets and long-lived consequences, incentives that ignore future risk are not neutral. They are extractive.

Structure Is Destiny

Governance structures do not guarantee good outcomes. But weak structures almost guarantee bad ones.

Boards that defer. Committees without authority. Incentives that reward speed over stewardship. Reporting that obscures more than it reveals.

These are not technical flaws. They are choices.

In real estate, governance structure determines whether sustainability is embedded or postponed, whether communities are engaged early or litigated later, and whether risk is managed or transferred to those with the least power to absorb it.

Governance is not about process for its own sake.

It is about deciding, in advance, who will be protected when decisions go wrong.

And they always do.

HOW ACCOUNTABILITY ACTUALLY WORKS

Accountability is not created by good intentions. It is created by friction.

Strong governance depends on whether conflicts are surfaced, challenged, and constrained. When accountability works, power is checked before damage is done. When it fails, problems are discovered only after trust is broken and value is lost.

In real estate, where relationships are dense and capital is concentrated, accountability is not automatic. It must be designed.

Conflicts of Interest Are the First Test
Conflicts of interest are not rare failures. They are structural risks.

A conflict exists when personal, financial, or professional incentives interfere with an individual's obligation to act in the organization's best interest. In real estate, this often appears quietly. A board member with outside development interests. An executive steering contracts toward affiliated firms. A decision that benefits insiders while externalizing risk.

The issue is not that conflicts arise. The issue is whether they are disclosed, reviewed, and constrained.

Effective governance requires mandatory disclosure of potential conflicts, independent review of related party transactions, and clear recusal requirements. These mechanisms slow decisions down. That is the point.

Without them, organizations drift toward self-dealing, even when no single actor intends harm. Stakeholders sense this quickly. Trust erodes long before violations are proven.

Accountability does not eliminate conflicts. It prevents them from becoming normalized.

Metrics Without Enforcement Are Theater
Governance frameworks are only as strong as the systems that enforce them.

Anti-corruption policies, ethics standards, and compliance rules are meaningless if violations carry no consequence. Accountability depends on detection, escalation, and protection for those who speak up.

Whistleblower programs matter because they bypass hierarchy. They create channels for truth to move upward when power blocks it. Without credible protection against retaliation, those channels remain unused.

Digital governance tools now play a larger role in this system. Platforms that track disclosures, incidents, and performance metrics reduce discretion and increase visibility. They do not replace judgment. They expose patterns that judgment alone often misses.

Metrics matter only when someone is responsible for acting on them.

Codes of Ethics Are Signals, Not Shields
Every organization has a Code of Ethics. The question is whether it is lived or laminated.

A Code of Ethics defines acceptable behavior, clarifies expectations, and sets boundaries. It establishes what the organization claims to value when tradeoffs arise. Conflicts of interest. Bribery. Fair treatment. Transparency.

But a code does not enforce itself.

Its real function is signaling. Internally, it tells employees what will be defended and what will not. Externally, it tells investors, regulators, and communities how seriously the organization treats its obligations.

When violations are ignored, selectively enforced, or quietly settled, the code becomes evidence against the organization rather than protection for it.

Accountability requires consistency. The same rules applied to senior leadership and junior staff. The same standards enforced in profitable moments and difficult ones.

Accountability Is About Consequences
Governance fails when accountability stops at documentation.
Policies without enforcement invite abuse. Metrics without consequences invite manipulation. Ethics without courage invite silence.

In real estate, accountability determines whether communities are consulted early or managed later through litigation. Whether safety violations are corrected or absorbed as costs. Whether long-term risk is addressed or transferred to those with the least power to resist.

Strong governance does not guarantee good outcomes. But weak accountability almost guarantees bad ones.

Accountability works when power is constrained, incentives are aligned, and consequences are real.

Everything else is performance.

DEI IN REAL ESTATE

This chapter is not about whether DEI is desirable. It is about what happens when governance systems are asked to absorb social goals without clear rules, accountability, or legitimacy.

Diversity, equity, and inclusion are not values statements. They are governance choices.

In real estate, DEI determines who is at the table when decisions are made, whose interests are represented in outcomes, and who absorbs risk when projects fail. It shapes tenant policy, hiring, procurement, community engagement, and capital allocation. Whether firms acknowledge it or not, DEI is already operating through governance systems. The question is whether it is designed intentionally or left to drift.

When DEI is embedded in governance, it strengthens decision-making and legitimacy. When it is bolted on without structure, it creates confusion, resentment, and legal risk.

Diversity Is About Representation With Authority

Diversity begins with representation, but it does not end there.

In governance, diversity matters only when it changes who has authority, not just who is present. Boards and leadership teams that reflect a narrow set of experiences tend to misread community risk, underestimate opposition, and repeat familiar mistakes. Real estate projects fail quietly at first and publicly later. Diversity helps surface blind spots early.

In practice, diversity in real estate governance means expanding who is recruited into leadership, construction, property management, and investment roles. It means widening pipelines into fields that have historically excluded women and underrepresented groups. It also means measuring representation and reporting it transparently.

Numbers alone do not solve governance failures. But homogeneity almost guarantees them.

Equity Is About Rules, Not Intentions
Equity is often misunderstood as equal treatment. In governance, equity is about fair rules applied to unequal starting points.

Real estate decisions distribute opportunity unevenly. Equity asks whether governance systems recognize that imbalance or reinforce it. This shows up in who gets hired, who gets trained, who is promoted, and who benefits economically from development.

Equitable governance requires structured pathways. Mentorship programs that are tied to advancement, not optics. Training and certification opportunities linked to real jobs, not symbolic inclusion. Hiring practices that prioritize local participation when developments reshape neighborhoods.

Equity also applies to tenants. Policies around affordability, accessibility, and enforcement determine whether housing is inclusive in practice or exclusionary by design.

Equity fails when it is treated as charity. It works when it is built into rules and incentives.

Inclusion Is About Power Being Exercised Differently
Inclusion is the most misused and least enforced part of DEI.

Inclusion does not mean asking for feedback after decisions are made. It means structuring decision-making so that affected groups have real influence before outcomes are locked in.

In real estate, inclusion shows up in how communities are engaged, not whether they are consulted. It shows up in whether employees can challenge unsafe or unethical practices without retaliation. It shows up in whether tenant data, complaints, and lived experience are taken seriously.

Governance enables inclusion by formalizing participation, documenting responses, and holding leadership accountable for how input is used. Inclusion without governance is performative. Governance without inclusion is brittle.

Why Governance Determines Whether DEI Works
DEI fails most often not because goals are wrong, but because governance is weak.

Without clear standards, DEI initiatives drift toward inconsistency. Without transparency, they invite suspicion. Without accountability, they collapse under pressure.

Strong governance aligns DEI goals with merit-based processes, stakeholder expectations, and long-term performance. It clarifies how decisions are made and why. It ensures that representation and qualifications are not treated as opposites, but as complementary requirements.

This matters more in real estate than in most industries. Housing, land use, and development decisions have long time horizons and uneven impacts. Governance choices made today shape outcomes for decades.

When DEI Lacks Governance, It Backfires

The 2019 lawsuit against the New York City Department of Education illustrates what happens when DEI goals are pursued without disciplined governance.

Leadership publicly emphasized representation while privately failing to apply consistent, merit-based processes. Hiring and promotion decisions lacked transparency. Accountability mechanisms failed. Perceptions of unfairness hardened into legal claims.

The result was a $2.1 million discrimination settlement and long-term damage to institutional credibility.

The lesson is not that DEI is dangerous. The lesson is that DEI without governance is unstable.

When standards are unclear, trust erodes. When processes are opaque, legitimacy collapses. When accountability is absent, costs surface elsewhere.

What DEI Governance Requires in Real Estate

Effective DEI governance in real estate is not complicated, but it is demanding.

Tenant policies must be fair, enforceable, and transparent. Community engagement must happen early and influence outcomes. Hiring and promotion processes must be documented and defensible. Leadership incentives must align with stated goals. Oversight must be real, not symbolic. Most importantly, governance must treat DEI as a system, not a slogan.

When designed well, DEI strengthens trust, reduces risk, and improves long-term performance. When designed poorly, it creates conflict, litigation, and reputational damage.

In real estate, the difference is not ideology.

It is governance.

GOVERNANCE CHALLENGES AND INNOVATION

Governance frameworks exist to impose discipline on decision-making. They are meant to slow organizations down just enough to ask hard questions before capital is committed, risk is transferred, or trust is spent. When they fail, the consequences are rarely abstract.

One recurring failure is financial mismanagement. This happens when growth outpaces oversight and debt replaces judgment. The collapse of Evergrande is not a mystery or a black swan. It was the predictable result of excessive leverage, weak internal controls, and a governance system that rewarded expansion without enforcing restraint. As debt accumulated, accountability thinned. When confidence broke, the entire structure collapsed. What failed was not the market alone. What failed was governance.

Another persistent challenge is weak ESG data and reporting. Many organizations talk about transparency while relying on incomplete, inconsistent, or unverifiable data. Without credible information, boards cannot evaluate risk, investors cannot price exposure, and regulators cannot distinguish performance from narrative. Poor data does not just limit disclosure. It undermines decision-making itself.

These failures point to a larger lesson. Governance cannot be a compliance exercise. It must function as an early warning system. It must anticipate risk, test assumptions, and constrain behavior before losses become irreversible.

Governance Innovations

Governance systems are now being reshaped by technology, not to replace judgment, but to support it.

Blockchain is one example. Its value is not novelty but structure. An immutable ledger reduces discretion where discretion creates risk. In real estate, blockchain can record ownership, document transactions, and verify compliance without relying solely on internal assurances. By reducing opacity, it limits the space where governance failures tend to grow.

Artificial intelligence is another tool reshaping governance. AI systems can aggregate operational data across portfolios, identify anomalies, and surface risks that would otherwise remain buried. Energy use, financial exposure, and compliance gaps can be monitored continuously rather than retrospectively. The benefit is not automation for its own sake. It is earlier intervention.

These tools do not solve governance problems on their own. They amplify the quality of oversight when leadership is willing to act on what the data reveals.

Evergrande as a Governance Stress Test

Evergrande illustrates what happens when governance fails to evolve alongside scale.

The company's central vulnerability was overleveraging. Strong governance would have imposed limits on debt accumulation and required stress testing against adverse market conditions. Clear debt thresholds and independent risk oversight could have slowed expansion before it became unsustainable.

Transparency failures compounded the problem. Adopting global reporting frameworks and enforcing internal audit discipline could have restored credibility earlier. Technologies such as blockchain could have strengthened confidence in financial disclosures by reducing ambiguity and manipulation.

Project feasibility was another weak point. Evergrande expanded rapidly without aligning development pace with real demand. Governance mechanisms that required independent feasibility reviews and environmental assessments could have constrained speculative growth. Simulation tools and scenario modeling could have tested assumptions before capital was locked in.

Board composition also mattered. A more independent board with financial and sustainability expertise could have challenged management decisions and enforced accountability. Digital governance tools could have improved information flow and decision transparency at the board level.

Stakeholder engagement was largely absent. Governance systems should create structured channels for investors, buyers, and communities to surface concerns before they become systemic risks. Digital platforms can support this, but only if leadership is willing to listen.

Regulatory compliance was treated as a constraint rather than a signal. Strong governance treats regulation as feedback. Compliance systems and predictive tools could have flagged regulatory exposure earlier and reduced shock.

Evergrande did not fail because innovation was unavailable. It failed because governance did not adapt.

Governance Pillar: What This Teaches Us

The governance pillar is not about formality. It is about alignment.

When financial incentives, information systems, and accountability structures pull in different directions, failure accelerates. When governance integrates transparency, discipline, and adaptive tools, risk becomes manageable.

Evergrande reminds us that growth without governance is fragility disguised as success. Innovation can strengthen governance, but only when institutions are willing to impose limits on themselves.

That is what governance is meant to do.

FROM FRAMEWORKS TO RESPONSIBILITY

By now, a pattern should be clear.

Environmental disasters do not arrive unannounced. Housing crises are not accidents. Governance failures rarely come out of nowhere. They are almost always preceded by ignored signals, misaligned incentives, and institutions that chose convenience over responsibility.

The Dust Bowl was not caused by weather alone. It was caused by policy. Cape Town's water crisis was not just about drought. It was about planning. Enron did not collapse because of bad luck. It collapsed because governance failed.

Real estate sits at the center of all of this.

It is where environmental limits meet human needs. Where capital meets communities. Where long-term value either gets built into the system or stripped out of it.

That is why frameworks matter.

HEADS UP exists because sustainability that does not account for people is incomplete. Housing, health, access, skills, data, infrastructure, and equity are not secondary issues. They are the outcomes that determine whether a project strengthens a place or destabilizes it.

STRIVE exists because intentions do not govern outcomes. Structures do. Strategy, transparency, resilience, innovation, values, and ethics are what separate real accountability from performative claims.

Social outcomes matters because history matters. Housing discrimination, redlining, displacement, and unequal access to opportunity are not relics of the past. They are embedded in today's market conditions. Ignoring that history does not make projects neutral. It makes them complicit.

Governance matters because power without accountability always drifts. Whether it is executive compensation, proxy voting, DEI initiatives, or financial leverage, governance determines whether systems correct themselves or compound their failures.

What ties all of this together is responsibility.

Not moral grandstanding. Not political signaling. Responsibility as in understanding the consequences of decisions made upstream. Responsibility as in building institutions that can absorb shocks rather than amplify them. Responsibility as in recognizing that markets work best when the rules are clear, the data is honest, and the human impacts are not externalized.

The most effective leaders I have observed are not ideological. They are pragmatic. They hold two ideas at once. That markets drive innovation, and that unchecked markets produce fragility. That growth matters, and that growth without trust eventually collapses.

This is not about choosing between profit and principle. That is a false choice. It is about aligning them.

Real estate will continue to shape how people live, work, age, and move. The question is whether it will do so deliberately or by default.

Frameworks like HEADS UP and STRIVE do not tell you what to think. They tell you where to look. They help you ask better questions. They make blind spots visible.

And in a world defined by climate risk, demographic shifts, technological change, and political fragmentation, asking the right questions is no longer optional. It is the work.

That is the work this book invites you to do.

GLOSSARY

Accountability: The condition under which decision-makers are answerable for outcomes, not just intentions. In this book, accountability means that risks, costs, and consequences remain connected to those who have the power to create them, rather than being shifted onto communities, workers, or future generations.

Affordable Housing: Housing for which total housing costs do not exceed 30 percent of a household's gross income. In practice, affordability is determined relative to Area Median Income and Fair Market Rent and is shaped as much by policy design as by market forces.

Area Median Income (AMI): The midpoint of household income in a defined geographic area, calculated annually by HUD. AMI is used to determine eligibility for housing programs and to structure affordability requirements, but it does not reflect lived cost burdens evenly across households.

Built Environment: The physical spaces created by human activity, including buildings, infrastructure, and land use systems. The built environment is where policy, capital, and daily life intersect, making it central to social, environmental, and economic outcomes.

Community Engagement: The process by which developers, owners, and institutions involve affected residents and stakeholders in planning and decision-making. In this book, engagement is treated as a legitimacy and risk issue, not a public relations exercise.

Conflict of Interest: A situation in which personal, financial, or professional incentives compromise objective decision-making. Effective governance requires disclosure, recusal, and independent oversight to prevent conflicts from distorting outcomes.

Disclosure: The act of reporting information about performance, risks, or practices. Disclosure alone does not create accountability. It becomes meaningful only when paired with clear standards, comparability, and consequences.

Diversity: The presence of varied identities, experiences, and perspectives within an organization or system. Diversity improves decision quality but only produces value when paired with equity and inclusion.

Double Materiality: A framework that considers both how sustainability issues affect financial performance and how organizational activities affect society and the environment. This book treats double materiality as a minimum baseline, not a complete answer.

Environmental, Social, and Corporate Governance (ESG): A broad category used to organize non-financial disclosure. In this book, ESG is treated as a reporting structure, not a strategy, and not a substitute for responsibility or outcomes.

Equity: The principle of fairness that accounts for unequal starting conditions. Equity focuses on removing structural barriers and aligning resources with need rather than treating all inputs as identical.

Externality: A cost or benefit created by a decision that is not reflected in its price. In real estate, externalities often appear as displacement, environmental damage, or infrastructure strain. This book treats externalities as evidence of misaligned accountability.

Fair Market Rent (FMR): An estimate published annually by HUD representing the cost of modest housing in a given area. FMR sets rent limits for housing assistance programs and reflects local market conditions rather than individual household affordability.

Framework: A structured way of organizing information to support better decision-making. Frameworks in this book are designed to reveal blind spots, not prescribe outcomes.

Governance: The systems, policies, and structures through which decisions are made and power is exercised. Governance determines whether markets self-correct or compound their failures.

Greenwashing: The practice of overstating or misrepresenting sustainability performance. Greenwashing flourishes where metrics are weak, accountability is absent, and incentives reward appearance over substance.

HEADS UP: A framework introduced in this book that centers Housing Affordability, Economic Access, Access to Health, Data Security, Skills and Human Capital, Urban Equity, and Public Infrastructure. It is designed to ensure that sustainability analysis accounts for lived outcomes rather than abstract metrics.

Inclusion: The condition in which diverse participants have real influence over decisions. Inclusion requires more than representation. It requires structures that allow voices to shape outcomes.

Materiality: The threshold at which an issue becomes significant enough to influence decisions. In this book, materiality is treated as dynamic and sector-specific rather than static or universal.

Proxy Voting: The mechanism by which shareholders vote on governance matters directly or through representatives. Proxy voting determines how values are translated into corporate action and where accountability ultimately resides.

Resilience: The capacity of systems to absorb shocks without cascading failure. In this book, resilience is not treated as a separate category but as an outcome embedded across environmental, social, and governance decisions.

Risk Transfer: The shifting of risk from decision-makers to other parties, often without consent or compensation. Many social and environmental failures in real estate result from deliberate or implicit risk transfer.

Sector Materiality: The recognition that different asset classes face distinct risks, impacts, and priorities. Sector materiality rejects one-size-fits-all disclosure and supports asset-specific accountability.

Social Capital: The value created through relationships, trust, and shared norms. Social capital shapes economic outcomes but is often ignored because it is difficult to quantify.

Social Contract: The implicit agreement between institutions and the people affected by their decisions. In real estate, the social contract governs legitimacy, consent, and long-term stability.

Stakeholder: Any individual or group affected by organizational decisions. This book treats stakeholders not as symbolic participants but as carriers of risk and value.

STRIVE: A framework introduced in this book focused on Strategy, Transparency, Resilience, Innovation, Values, and Ethics. STRIVE emphasizes that outcomes are governed by structure, not intent.

Universal Design: An approach to design that makes spaces usable by the widest possible range of people without adaptation. Universal design is a practical expression of equity in the built environment.

Urban Renewal: A mid-twentieth-century policy framework that used public power to redevelop cities, often through displacement. Its legacy shapes present-day housing markets and trust dynamics.

Workforce Housing: Housing intended for moderate-income households who earn too much to qualify for subsidies but too little to afford market-rate housing. Workforce housing is essential to economic stability and regional competitiveness.

ABOUT THE AUTHOR

Suhail Y Tayeb is Director of the Center for the Sustainable Built Environment at New York University, where he leads research and teaching at the intersection of real estate, governance, policy, and long-term value creation in the built environment.

A developer, investor, and educator with more than twenty-five years of experience across residential and commercial real estate, Suhail has guided projects through the full investment and development lifecycle. His work focuses on how decisions about land, capital, regulation, and institutional design shape social outcomes, market behavior, and risk in real assets.

At NYU, he teaches graduate and undergraduate courses on real estate systems, governance, and sustainable development, and leads applied research on performance measurement, accountability, and decision frameworks used by investors, operators, and policymakers. He also directs the development of applied dashboards and analytical tools that examine how real estate decisions translate into measurable outcomes across portfolios and cities.

Suhail is the chair of NYU's annual Conference on Sustainable Real Estate, which convenes leaders from industry, policy, and academia to examine the tradeoffs, constraints, and governance challenges shaping the future of development. His work and teaching extend globally, including advisory and research engagements in the United States, Europe, and the Middle East.

He holds a Sloan Master's degree in Leadership and Strategy from London Business School and a Bachelor's degree in Electrical and Computer Engineering and Computer Science from the University of Wisconsin–Madison. His work spans real estate governance, social impact, AI-enabled infrastructure, and the institutional forces that determine how the built environment evolves.

For inquiries related to research, advisory engagements, or speaking, he can be reached at info@SuhailYTayeb.com.

OTHER BOOKS BY THE AUTHOR

Profitable and Sustainable Real Estate Investing: An Investor's Guide

The 25 Steps to Accurate Property Valuation: How to value property faster and easier than you've ever imagined!

REFERENCES

This book draws on a wide body of work across real estate, governance, political economy, social policy, and institutional design. The sources listed below reflect the ideas, frameworks, and case logic that inform the analysis, rather than serving as a comprehensive bibliography.

Real estate decisions are not made in isolation. They emerge from layers of law, finance, policy, and organizational incentives, and their consequences are felt by people who often had little influence over those choices. Much of what appears in these pages comes from practice, observation, and engagement with real projects, institutions, and communities, as well as from working inside the systems that shape the built environment.

The works cited here provide grounding for readers who wish to explore the intellectual foundations behind questions of power, accountability, and long-term value in real assets. They are included not to settle debates, but to help readers see how different disciplines have tried, often imperfectly, to explain how decisions get made and why their consequences endure.

- Coleman, James S. "Social Capital in the Creation of Human Capital." American Journal of Sociology 94 (1988): S95–S120.
- Edmans, Alex. "Does the Stock Market Fully Value Intangibles? Employee Satisfaction and Equity Prices." Journal of Financial Economics 101, no. 3 (2011): 621–640.
- Elkington, John. Cannibals with Forks: The Triple Bottom Line of 21st Century Business. Oxford: Capstone Publishing, 1998.
- Friedman, Milton. "The Social Responsibility of Business Is to Increase Its Profits." The New York Times Magazine, September 13, 1970.
- Global Reporting Initiative (GRI). GRI Standards. Amsterdam: Global Reporting Initiative, various years.
- International Financial Reporting Standards Foundation. International Sustainability Disclosure Standards (ISSB). London: IFRS Foundation, 2021–present.
- Materiality Map Project. Understanding Financially Material ESG Issues. Sustainability Accounting Standards Board (SASB).
- Sustainability Accounting Standards Board (SASB). Industry Standards. San

Francisco: SASB, 2018.
- Task Force on Climate-related Financial Disclosures (TCFD). Recommendations of the Task Force on Climate-related Financial Disclosures. Financial Stability Board, 2017.
- United Nations. The Sustainable Development Goals. New York: United Nations, 2015.
- United Nations Principles for Responsible Investment (UN PRI). Six Principles for Responsible Investment. United Nations, 2006.
- Sullivan, Leon H. The Global Sullivan Principles of Social Responsibility. United Nations, 1999. U.S. Department of Housing and Urban Development (HUD). Area Median Income and Fair Market Rent Documentation. Washington, DC, various years.
- U.S. Federal Trade Commission. Green Guides for the Use of Environmental Marketing Claims. Washington, DC, 1992, updated editions.
- European Commission. Corporate Sustainability Reporting Directive (CSRD). Brussels, 2022.
- Global Real Estate Sustainability Benchmark (GRESB). GRESB Real Estate Assessment Framework. Amsterdam, various years.
- Greenhouse Gas Protocol. Corporate Accounting and Reporting Standard. World Resources Institute and World Business Council for Sustainable Development, revised edition.
- National Endowment for the Arts. Markusen, Ann, and Anne Gadwa. Creative Placemaking. Washington, DC, 2010.
- Edwards, Michael. Civil Society. Cambridge: Polity Press, 2009.
- Harvey, David. Social Justice and the City. Baltimore: Johns Hopkins University Press, 1973.
- Jacobs, Jane. The Death and Life of Great American Cities. New York: Random House, 1961.
- New York City Department of City Planning. Essex Crossing Project Documentation. New York, various years.
- New York State Energy Research and Development Authority (NYSERDA). Multifamily Performance Program. Albany, NY.
- U.S. Occupational Safety and Health Administration (OSHA). Workplace Safety and Training Standards. Washington, DC.
- European Union Agency for Cybersecurity (ENISA). Cybersecurity Risk Management for Infrastructure Sectors. Brussels.
- Morningstar Sustainalytics. ESG Risk Ratings Methodology. Chicago.
- MSCI. ESG Ratings Methodology. New York.
- Moody's ESG Solutions. Climate and ESG Risk Integration. New York.

www.ingramcontent.com/pod-product-compliance
Lightning Source LLC
LaVergne TN
LVHW022117200926
848481LV00003B/1182